A Practical Guide to Teaching Citizenship in the Secondary School

This practical and accessible workbook is designed to support student teachers as they develop their basic teaching skills, and increase their broader knowledge and understanding for teaching citizenship. Newly qualified and beginning teachers should also find it useful.

A Practical Guide to Teaching Citizenship in the Secondary School provides a wealth of practical activities and materials, underpinned by relevant theory, which have been developed through the author's experience of working with student teachers. These activities provide opportunities to analyse learning and performance. The book has been designed to be written in directly, and so provide a useful record of progress. Case studies are also included, as are examples of existing good practice and a range of tried-and-tested strategies.

The book has been written to complement *Learning to Teach Citizenship in the Secondary School: A Companion to School Experience* (also published by Routledge), and can be used to reinforce some of the basic teaching skills covered in this textbook. However, the book can also be used equally successfully as a stand-alone text. It has been designed to be used by student teachers, on their own or with others, or by school- or university-based tutors with their student teachers, to develop and/or reinforce their understanding about some of the important aspects of learning to teach citizenship.

Liam Gearon is Professor of Education at Roehampton University, UK. He is the founder and former director of the Centre for Research in Human Rights in the School of Education Studies and Senior Fellow at the Crucible Centre, School of Business and Social Sciences, also at Roehampton University, UK.

Routledge Teaching Guides
Series Editors: Susan Capel and Marilyn Leask

These Practical Guides are to run alongside the **Learning to Teach (subject) in the Secondary School**.

A Practical Guide to Teaching Physical Education in the Secondary School
Edited by *Susan Capel, Peter Breckon and Jean O'Neill*

A Practical Guide to Teaching History in the Secondary School
Edited by *Martin Hunt*

A Practical Guide to Teaching Modern Foreign Languages in the Secondary School
Edited by *Norbert Pachler and Ana Redondo*

A Practical Guide to Teaching ICT in the Secondary School
Edited by *Steve Kennewell*

These Practical Guides have been designed as companions to **Learning to Teach (subject) in the Secondary School**. For information on the Routledge Teaching Guides series please visit our website at www.routledge.com/education

A Practical Guide to Teaching Citizenship in the Secondary School

Edited by
Liam Gearon

Routledge
Taylor & Francis Group

LONDON AND NEW YORK

First published 2007
by Routledge
2 Park Square, Milton Park, Abingdon, Oxon OX14 4RN

Simultaneously published in the USA and Canada
by Routledge
270 Madison Ave, New York, NY 10016

Routledge is an imprint of the Taylor & Francis Group, an informa business

© 2007 Liam Gearon for editorial matter and selection. Individual chapters,
the contributors.

Typeset in Palatino by
Keystroke, 28 High St, Tettenhall, Wolverhampton
Printed and bound in Great Britain by
Bell & Bain Ltd, Glasgow

British Library Cataloguing in Publication Data
A catalogue record for this book is available from the British Library

Library of Congress Cataloging in Publication Data
A catalog record for this book has been requested

ISBN10: 0–415–36741–7 (pbk)
ISBN10: 0–203–01979–2 (ebk)

ISBN13: 978–0–415–36741–7 (pbk)
ISBN13: 978–0–203–01979–5 (ebk)

Contents

Series Editors' Introduction

This practical workbook is part of a series of textbooks for student teachers. It complements and extends the popular textbook entitled *Learning to Teach in the Secondary School: A Companion to School Experience*, as well as the subject-specific textbook *Learning to Teach Citizenship in the Secondary School*. We anticipate that you will want to use this book in conjunction with these other texts.

Teaching is rapidly becoming a more research- and evidence-informed profession. We have used research and professional evidence about what makes good practice to underpin the 'Learning to Teach in the Secondary School' series and these practical workbooks. Both the generic and the subject-specific books in the series provide theoretical, research and professional evidence-based advice and guidance to support you as you focus on developing aspects of your teaching or your pupils' learning as you progress through your initial teacher education course and beyond. Although the generic and subject-specific books include some case studies and tasks to help you consider the issues, the practical application of material is not their major focus. That is the role of this book.

This book aims to reinforce your understanding of aspects of your teaching, support you in aspects of your development as a teacher and your teaching and enable you to analyse your success as a teacher in maximising pupils' learning by focusing on practical applications. The practical activities in this book can be used in a number of ways. Some activities are designed to be undertaken by you individually, others as a joint task in pairs and yet others as group work working with, for example, other student teachers or a school- or university-based tutor. Your tutor may use the activities with a group of student teachers. The book has been designed so that you can write directly into it.

In England, new ways of working for teachers are being developed through an initiative remodelling the school workforce. This may mean that you have a range of colleagues to support in your classroom. They also provide an additional resource on which you can draw. In any case, you will, of course, need to draw on additional resources to support your development and the *Learning to Teach in the Secondary School, 4th edition* website (http://www.routledge.com/textbooks/0415363926) lists key websites for Scotland, Wales, Northern Ireland and England. For example, key websites relevant to teachers in England include the Teacher Training Resource Bank (www.ttrb.ac.uk). Others include: www.teachernet.gov.uk. which is part of the DfES schools web initiative; www.becta.org.uk, which has ICT resources; and www.qca.org.uk. which is the Qualifications and Curriculum Authority website.

We do hope that this practical workbook will be useful in supporting your development as a teacher.

Susan Capel
Marilyn Leask
April 2006

Contributors

Hilary Cremin is Director, Centre for Citizenship Studies in Education (CCSE), School of Education, University of Leicester.

Ian Davies is Reader in Educational Studies at the University of York. He is the author of numerous articles and books about citizenship education. He is the Deputy Director of Citized (www.citized.info), which includes a role as the editor of the journal *Citizenship Teaching and Learning*. He has extensive international experience in citizenship projects.

Liam Gearon is Professor of Education, School of Education, founder and former Director, Centre for Research in Human Rights, and Senior Fellow in the Crucible Centre for Education in Citizenship, Human Rights and Social Justice, School of Business and Social Sciences, Roehampton University. The author and editor of numerous books in literature, study of religion and education, he is Chair of the Association of University Lecturers in Religion and Education (UK) and Regional Vice-President of the International Human Rights Education Consortium, whose secretariat is based at Utica College in New York.

Jeremy Hayward is Lecturer in Education (Citizenship), Institute of Education, University of London.

Darius Jackson is Lecturer in History and Citizenship in Education at the School of Education, University of Birmingham. Prior to this he taught for nineteen years in a range of comprehensive schools in Gloucestershire and Birmingham. He has been a Head of History for eleven years as well as working in a number of teams leading whole-school initiatives in raising pupil attainment, primary-secondary links, literacy and thinking skills.

Lee Jerome is Course Leader for the History with Citizenship PGCE at Anglia Ruskin University, where he also teaches about education policy and inclusion. His research interests include the use of debate in secondary schools, strategies for promoting active citizenship in schools and the relationship between citizenship education and people's ideas about democracy. Before taking up his current post Lee was Education Director at the Institute for Citizenship, where he managed a variety of projects with schools and produced a range of resources for teachers. He originally trained as a social studies teacher and taught history and sociology in London for six years.

Ralph Leighton is Senior Lecturer in Education and subject leader for PGCE Citizenship at Canterbury Christ Church University. Having had a number of jobs before leaving Scotland to become a student then a social worker in London, he taught sociology and other subjects during a twenty-two-year career in Kent schools. A successful head of department and faculty manager, he had responsibility for curriculum change and for staff development as a member of his school's senior management team. He has been involved in public examination work for over twenty years, most recently as a chief examiner, as well as teaching part time in further and higher education. His current research interests relate to the processes and experiences involved in making citizenship teachers, and in the potential for social change inherent in citizenship education.

Sandie Llewellin is Lecturer in the Graduate School of Education at the University of Bristol, where she is responsible for the Secondary PGCE Citizenship course.

Russell Manning is Lecturer in History in Education at the School of Education, University of Birmingham. Prior to this he taught for eleven years in a comprehensive school in Dudley. He was Head of History as well as holding a range of academic and pastoral middle-management posts.

Mary Richardson is studying for a Ph.D. in the Centre for Research in Beliefs, Rights and Values at Roehampton University and teaches on the BA Education Programme.

Paul Warwick is currently the Deputy Director of the Centre for Citizenship Studies in Education at the University of Leicester. He has worked in the field of education over the last 10 years developing participatory approaches to Education for Citizenship and Sustainable Development. His research interests include: action research as a tool for change, student voice in education, and approaches towards working with hard to reach learners.

Liz West is a Senior Lecturer in History and Citizenship at St Martin's College, Carlisle. Prior to this she was an Assistant Headteacher in a large city-based comprehensive school where she led a training school. She has contributed to articles on developing subject knowledge in citizenship within Citized and is the author of several chapters for a citizenship GCSE textbook. She is currently involved in a European project developing training materials on using assessment for teaching and learning.

Chapter 1   What is citizenship education?

IAN DAVIES

INTRODUCTION

What is citizenship education? This could be one of the most difficult questions that teachers in their role as subject specialists will ever have to face (and certainly a lot more difficult than 'What is maths education?' or 'What is history education?', where – despite many controversies and uncertainties – there is much greater consensus about what needs to be taught and learned and long-established processes for encouraging learning). This chapter draws attention to some of the debates and issues that are raging (and have raged for a very long time) about citizenship and whether (and, if so, how) it can be taught and learned. A range of examples will be given of practical activities that could be used in schools and elsewhere and you will be invited to consider what you think is the essence of 'real' citizenship education. My view about the nature of citizenship and citizenship education will be declared in this chapter but, of course, this is not the only perspective that is possible. This one brief chapter is certainly not enough to do any more than begin to scratch the surface of this complex field.

OBJECTIVES

By the end of this chapter you should be able to:

- Understand the key ideas about citizenship.
- Understand the current meaning of citizenship education as part of the National Curriculum for England.
- Understand the issues in the relationship between citizenship and citizenship education
- Be able critically to review educational activities for their suitability for use in a citizenship education programme.

Despite all the controversy, the answer to the question 'What is citizenship education?' is, in one sense, easy. The National Curriculum for Citizenship in England was developed following the Crick Report (DfEE/QCA 1998). That report characterised citizenship education as consisting of social and moral responsibility, community involvement and political literacy. The report declared its principal aim in very ambitious terms:

> We aim at no less than a change in the political culture of this country both nationally and locally: for people to think of themselves as active citizens, willing, able and equipped to have an influence in public life and with the critical capacities to weigh

evidence before speaking and acting; to build on and to extend radically to young people the best in existing traditions of community involvement and public service and to make them individually confident in finding new forms of involvement and action among themselves.

(DfEE/QCA 1998, pp. 7–8)

The National Curriculum Order for citizenship became compulsory for secondary schools in England in September 2002. The following indicates the three key aspects of the requirements:

Teaching should ensure that *knowledge and understanding* about becoming informed citizens are acquired and applied when developing *skills of enquiry and communication*, and *participation and responsible action*.

(DfEE/QCA 1999, p. 14; emphasis added)

The assessment of citizenship education is compulsory but the uncertainty surrounding the area has meant that for the one attainment target that has been established levels have not been declared as in other subjects. Instead brief end-of-key-stage descriptions are given for key stages 3 and 4.

There is support for the implementation of citizenship education. Citizenship teams have been established within the DfES (Department for Education and Skills) and QCA (Qualifications and Curriculum Authority). The Association for Citizenship Teaching (ACT) has been established, and schemes of work have been produced by the QCA. The Training and Development Agency for Schools (TDA) is funding a project (see www.citized.info) designed to strengthen action in teacher education for citizenship education. Almost all educational publishers active in the schools sector have rushed to produce materials for the new commercial market in citizenship education.

So, if we focus on the practical details of what is required by law to be taught, then a simple answer can be given to the question 'What is citizenship education?' But even in this fairly straightforward situation the context in real schools and with real teachers and learners is potentially problematic. It would be wrong to imagine that government policy documents will tell us what is really being implemented. Early evaluation and inspection reports point to a range of challenges being faced by schools (Kerr *et al.* 2003), including the delivery of citizenship education through Personal and Social Education (PSE) which Crick (2001) had explicitly warned against, and teacher uncertainty about the implementation process.

In light of controversy over the heart of citizenship education and uncertainty over how it can be practically implemented, I show below a number of activities that can be used to consider ways to identify citizenship and citizenship education.

Activity 1.1 What does citizenship mean?

Two quotations about citizenship are shown below. They show very different perspectives about citizenship. Before you read the quotations and do an activity related to them, please consider the very clear summary of citizenship that can be found in Heater (1999). In that book Heater discusses the two main traditions from which our current understandings about citizenship have been drawn: the liberal (rights based and often related to individuals who are wary of state power) and the civic republican (emphasising duties and recognising the need for the power of the state to ensure that there is some measure of equality). Heater argues (convincingly, in my view) that it is unnecessary to see these two traditions as being mutually exclusive:

Activity 1.1 *continued*

. . . by being a virtuous, community-conscious participant in civic affairs (a republican requirement), a citizen benefits by enhancing his or her own individual development (a liberal objective). Citizenship does not involve an either/or choice.

(Heater 1999, p. 177)

However, knowledge of these two traditions does allow us to see where people are coming from when they discuss citizenship. Now, please think about the questions shown below in relation to the two quotations that appear after them.

Questions to consider: Who do you think was the author of each of the quotations given below? Can you make an informed guess as to what sort of people they are? What sort of jobs do they do? What sort of views about citizenship do they hold? Why do you think they hold those particular views? What sort of traditions relate most closely to the perspectives given in the quotations? What sort of work that could be undertaken within or outside school would emerge from the two different approaches represented in the quotations? Which of the two quotations (or what sort of blend between the two quotations) do you prefer and why?

Quotation 1

Active citizenship is the free acceptance by individuals of voluntary obligations to the community of which they are members. It cannot be conjured up by legislation or by political speeches – although both can help. It arises from traditions of civic obligations and voluntary service which are central to the thinking of this government and rooted in our history.

Quotation 2

The practice of citizenship is about ensuring everybody the entitlements necessary to the exercise of their liberty. As a political question welfare is about rights, not caring, and the history of citizenship has been the struggle to make freedom real, not to tie us all in the leading strings of therapeutic good intentions.

Sources

The reference for Quotation 1 is D. Hurd (1988) 'Freedom Will Flourish where Citizens Accept Responsibility', *Independent*, 13 February. Douglas Hurd was a key member of several of Margaret Thatcher's governments. At the time he made that statement he was at the Home Office and was therefore responsible for law and order and immigration. His junior minister at the time, John Patten, would later become Secretary of State for Education and be closely involved with the attempt to implement a form of citizenship education in the early 1990s that emphasised the need for young people to volunteer.

The reference for Quotation 2 is M. Ignatieff (1989) 'Citizenship and Moral Narcissism', *Political Quarterly*, 60, 1. Michael Ignatieff is a philosopher, writer and politician. One of his recent books is titled *Human Rights* (edited by Amy Gutman and published by Princeton University Press in 2001). Ignatieff has been Director of the Carr Center for Human Rights Policy at Harvard University and is (2006) a Liberal party member in the Canadian parliament.

One of the key ways of characterising citizenship is to focus on the relationship between the individual and the state. An obvious way of considering that relationship is by investigating voting patterns in general elections. The following activity allows you to consider the meaning of citizenship and its relationship with the sorts of things that should or could be done by teachers and learners.

Activity 1.2   Understanding political participation (or, 'Do we live in a democracy?')

You are about to see some data from recent elections. Please consider this data and ask yourself three questions (perhaps you could discuss with some colleagues or friends):

- Do you feel concerned as a result of seeing the information about voting patterns in elections? Why? Why not?
- Do you feel that this information should be of particular interest to teachers? Why? Why not?
- Do you think that knowledge of this information should lead to the provision of a particular sort of citizenship education? Why? Why not?

The 2005 General Election

Party	Seats in Parliament	Share of total electorate
Labour	356	22%
Conservative	197	20%
Liberal Democrat	62	14%
Others	30	6%

Share of total electorate for winning prime minister and party

Prime Minister	Share of total electorate
Churchill 1951 (Conservative)	41%
Wilson 1974 (Labour)	29%
Thatcher 1983 (Conservative)	32%
Major 1992 (Conservative)	33%
Blair 1997 (Labour)	32%
Blair 2001 (Labour)	25%
Blair 2005 (Labour)	22%

Activity 1.2 *continued*

What do the data about voting mean?

When reviewing the information about elections people have very different reactions. Some suggest that there is a huge crisis in society and that unless we act now the alienation from constitutional politics will increase to a point where hardly anyone will bother to vote. Teachers, it is argued, must step in and encourage young people to vote. Others adopt a different view. They suggest that there is little to worry about. People may not vote when they are young but as they get older they will start to vote; not voting when the result of an election seems a foregone conclusion is simply a sensible action and nothing to worry about; people can express their dissatisfaction with their preferred political party by not voting (as opposed to voting for a party that they do not like). Young people and others are very interested in political issues (although they do not want to see middle-aged men argue about procedural points in the House of Commons). If teachers encourage young people to vote, are they allowing themselves to act as the agents of party politicians and not being educators? What do you think? Remember the three questions that were given at the beginning of this activity as you develop your answers to these questions. (You might want to look at more data about elections. If so, please go to the website of the electoral commission (http://www. electoralcommission.org.uk).)

There are many debates about citizenship and teachers must think carefully about what they want to focus on.

Activity 1.3 Where do we draw the boundaries around citizenship education? How do we know when we are teaching citizenship?

An argument is made below for a particular approach to citizenship education. Read the argument and then discuss with others whether you agree or not.

Some argue that citizenship encompasses everything. Audigier (1998, p. 13):

> Since the citizen is an informed and responsible person, capable of taking part in public debate and making choices, nothing of what is human should be unfamiliar to him [*sic*], nothing of what is experienced in society should be foreign to democratic citizenship.

Audigier is asking us to realise the very broad nature of what it means to be a citizen. We cannot turn away from anything that involves social justice – and that involves just about everything. But he is also giving a warning to teachers. It would not be helpful if a teacher were to be presented with a syllabus that asked for everything to be taught! So, there must be limits. Some people claim that those limits can be achieved by the application of specific perspectives. Isin and Wood (1999) argue for an identity-based citizenship. Osler and Vincent (2002) declare that global education is the way forward. Crick (2000) asserts the need for a political knowledge and activity in everyday life. Arnot and Dillabough (2002) emphasise feminist perspectives. These perspectives (broad and precise) may all be legitimate but it is important to focus attention on educational issues. It is vitally important to consider the nature of citizenship (if we did not do this we would have nothing to teach at all) but just as history teachers have a different role from historians and science teachers have a different role from scientists, we need to focus on the nature of learning that we think is desirable and what sort of teaching is required to achieve those outcomes.

In light of the above it is necessary to ask what is it that people need to learn *about* citizenship and, more important, what it is they need to know and do in order to *be* citizens. Learners should go beyond learning content, and should develop understanding dispositions and abilities associated with:

- Rationality grounded in a critical appreciation of social and political realities.
- Respect for diversity within the context of a pluralistic democracy.
- Participation arising from an acceptance of one's social and political responsibilities and appreciation of one's own rights and entitlements.

Using this emphasis on procedural matters it would be possible to write classroom resources that used the 'content' of, for example, justice, identity or equality but the key focus would be to encourage students to act as citizens. So there would be a relationship between the business of students acting as citizens (explaining, participating, respecting) in ways that allowed them to understand citizenship (and its key concepts such as justice, equality, etc.), and this would have meaning in public situations. A lesson that was 'merely' about the private acts of an individual (being kind, living healthily, applying for a job, etc.) would not count, in my view, as citizenship education. This is not to say that getting a job, being happy, healthy and living a good life are not important. But citizenship education is not the same as personal and social and health education. When working on citizenship education in the way that has been described above, students would need:

- to explain their views, their understandings and their arguments about citizenship;
- to respect others, accommodate and reflect upon opinions and views that may be different from their own when considering citizenship;
- to participate in the consideration and debate of these ideas in the classroom and (ideally) use this experience and understanding in their life outside school.

Activity 1.4 What sort of work with young people can be called citizenship education?

What, then, would count as a citizenship lesson or activity? The way to answer this question is to think about the types of concept that are being explored and what sorts of things students are being asked to do. Look at the list of activities shown below and after discussion with a friend or colleague give your responses to the following:

- Is the activity an example of citizenship education – yes? no? possibly? What are your reasons for your decision?
- Would you want to be involved in the development of this sort of work as described here? Explain your answer.
- Can you suggest any improvements (especially to those activities that you deem not to be citizenship education) in order to make it relevant to the work of a citizenship teacher?

Activity 1.4 *continued*

Activities

- A teacher organises a charity walk by year 10 students to raise money for the victims of a natural disaster. Students collect sponsorship money. There is an assembly in which the nature of the disaster is explained and examples are given of how the money will help. A representative of a charity arrives in the assembly to receive a cheque and to thank the students for their work. By their work, she says, the students have helped in a very real way to make the world a better place.

- A lesson on the dangers of smoking includes a discussion about individual health risks. Students are invited to prepare questions to put to health workers who visit their class. The questions focus on the experiences of working with people who have become seriously ill as a direct consequence of active or passive smoking. Following the visit of the health workers students develop ideas for posters that would encourage people to stop smoking.

- A video is shown about sexually transmitted diseases. Students are informed about the different types of disease and their symptoms. A teacher advises students to think about their responsibilities in the context of the need for high moral standards. The teacher uses the phrase 'the personal is political' during the time he is encouraging students to act sensibly. He urges the young people to think about their future and suggests that life will be easier for them if they are able to learn important lessons about responsibility.

- A school council is established. The student chair of the council prepares a proposal to abolish school uniform. The resulting discussion at the council meeting includes consideration of the likely views of parents, the value of a school identity gained through uniform, the relationship between using different types of clothing and discipline in the school. The head makes it clear that she will not accept abolition of the existing uniform. The chair of the council resigns. There is some evidence of discontent (largely in the form of negative comments from students to teachers) about the way this matter has been handled.

- A local council has decided that it would like to consult local residents about how part of its budget should be spent in the forthcoming year. A meeting takes place between a councillor and the citizenship co-ordinator of a local school. Year 9 pupils are asked to complete a questionnaire in a citizenship lesson to show their views about how the money should be spent. Small groups of year 9 students deliver questionnaires to addresses near to the school. A sample of the completed questionnaires is given to the students to analyse. They are asked to summarise the responses from different age groups and from men and women. They are asked to comment on the questionnaire that was used. Finally, they draw up recommendations to be considered by the council.

SUMMARY

We will probably never have complete agreement about the nature of citizenship. In a democracy that is probably no bad thing. We need ongoing debate and redefinition. However, confusion and lack of conceptual clarity are unhelpful. The activities shown above will help to clear away some of the smoke around the heat of the citizenship debate. We need people to understand citizenship and to be citizens and more than anything else this involves direct connection with action that relates to key concepts about social justice in public contexts.

REFERENCES

Arnot, M. and Dillabough, J.-A. (2002) *Challenging Democracy: international perspectives on gender, education and citizenship*. London, Routledge.

Audigier, F. (1998) *Basic Concepts and Core Competences of Education for Democratic Citizenship: an initial consolidated report*. Strasbourg, Council of Europe.

Crick, B. (2000) *Essays on Citizenship*. London, Continuum.

—— (2001) Preface. In Arthur, J., Davies, I., Wrenn, A., Haydn, T. and Kerr, D. (eds), *Citizenship through Secondary History*. London, RoutledgeFalmer.

Department for Education and Employment/QCA (1998) *Education for Citizenship and the Teaching of Democracy in Schools. Final report of the Advisory Group on Citizenship*. [The Crick Report]. London, DfEE/QCA.

—— (1999) *Citizenship: Key Stages 3–4*. London, DfEE/QCA.

Heater, D. (1999) *What is Citizenship?* Cambridge, Polity Press.

Isin, E. F. and Wood, P. K. (1999) *Citizenship and Identity*. London, Sage.

Kerr, D., Cleaver, E., Ireland, E. and Blenkinsop, S. (2003) *Citizenship Education Longitudinal Study. First cross-sectional survey 2001–2*. Norwich, HMSO.

Osler, A. and Vincent, K. (2002) *Citizenship and the Challenge of Global Education*. Stoke on Trent, Trentham.

Chapter 2   Values, beliefs and the citizenship teacher

JEREMY HAYWARD

INTRODUCTION

Citizenship teaching involves exploring the central political and moral debates of the day. It also involves promoting key values. It is vital for the citizenship teacher to be clear about the role of values in teaching. However, this area is itself controversial and clarity is not easily achieved. This chapter does not attempt to give a definitive account on such issues; it is simply designed to provoke thought so you may clarify your own position.

OBJECTIVES

By the end of this chapter you should be able to:

- Reflect on the nature of values and their role in education.
- Highlight the values underpinning citizenship teaching.
- Identify ways in which values of citizenship can be undermined by the teaching methods.
- Evaluate different strategies for teaching controversial issues.

VALUES AND BELIEFS

'Every art and every investigation, and similarly every action and pursuit, is considered to aim at some good'.

(Aristotle)

The concept of *values* is not easy to define. The term is used fairly loosely and covers a range of purposes. Values can refer to those elements of life we consider worth pursuing: for example, happiness, freedom and justice. The term can also refer to the dispositions and character traits considered important to develop or maintain, such as courage, honesty and compassion.

The focus of this chapter will be on the practical relevance of values in relation to education and in relation to the citizenship classroom in particular. As such, a prolonged theoretical discussion on the nature of values will be avoided. However, it is worth briefly visiting the philosophical arena, if only to draw out one or two features of values that will be salient to future discussion.[1]

A common distinction drawn is that between statements of fact and statements of values. Factual statements attempt to describe how the world is. They are descriptive in nature. Values statements describe how the world *ought* to be. They are *prescriptive* in nature. As prescriptions, values underpin our answers to the general moral question of *How should we live our lives?*

Not all values need be moral, however. You might value humour whereas a friend might not, neither of you wishing to claim that your liking or otherwise had moral status. In this chapter I will be concerned only with moral values, noting however that the distinction between more personal preferences and social and public values is not always clear.

It is claimed that values of some kind underpin our every action. The suggestion, following Aristotle, is that that all our actions are focused on goals or ends, which in turn will represent values and value judgements. For example, Ben might find himself walking down the road with the goal of going to a shop. However, simply arriving at the shop is not Ben's ultimate goal. In this case, he entered the shop to buy a razor. Yet even this is still a means to some other end, namely to shave. Shaving in turn is a means to avoid the itching sometimes created by a beard. Here perhaps we reach the ultimate end or goal – physical comfort. So Ben's walking down the road on that occasion was driven by the fact that one of his values is physical comfort.

Through analysing our everyday activity it is claimed that we can show that all of our actions are aimed at something we personally consider worthwhile or that we value. However, the fact that Ben values physical comfort is unlikely to have been a conscious thought in his mind as he walked down the street. Only by reflection might he realise the values that underpinned his action. This raises the question of how we know what our own values are.

One simple way of finding out might be to ask someone. This would reveal their conscious deliberations on the subject. Another way would be to observe a person closely over a period of time and analyse their actions. Sometimes these two indicators may be at odds. For example, a person may verbally claim to value the environment, yet fail in their everyday life to reduce, repair, reuse, recycle or indeed act in any way that would help to achieve their consciously stated value. Does this person really value the environment as they claim to?

It is a matter of philosophical debate whether behaviour or consciously expressed thought should act as the ultimate compass of a person's beliefs. However, the distinction, as will be discussed below, is of practical relevance to the citizenship classroom.

In many cases moral beliefs will amount to more or less the same thing as moral values. If you value personal freedom, you are likely to sign up to the corresponding moral belief that personal freedom is a good thing.

Moral and political beliefs may also have a different function from values. For example, two people may both value social justice and may agree on the need to reduce global poverty. However, they may disagree as to how this could be best achieved. One may favour direct aid; the other may claim this is counter-productive and advocate greater spending on education. The two share the same value but have different beliefs as to how these values could be best realised.

RELATIVISM, VALUES AND EDUCATION

History is not short of societies claiming to be in moral crisis. Our present society is no exception. Citing a range of factors such as the increasing diversity of society, the pluralism of values and the post-modern suggestion that human thought and language prevent access to any ultimate truths, some commentators suggest that we now live in a society where moral truth is impossible and in which all moral beliefs are deemed equally valid.

It is claimed that this modern, 'relativist' society has forced schools to play a very different role in relation to the teaching of values. 'From being an important mechanism by which norms and codes were transmitted, they have become the cockpit in which the conflicts [of values] are first encountered by the young' (Tomlinson 1995: 310).

If we are to accept that we now live in a new intellectual and social climate where a plurality of values exists, does this mean schools should no longer promote values?

It certainly appears true that many people are less comfortable with the idea of schools or teachers transmitting values than perhaps they were sixty years ago. This concern is acknowledged in the Crick Report: 'Parents and the public generally may be worried about the possibility of bias and indoctrination in teaching about citizenship' (QCA 1998: 8). It has also been suggested that the more liberal-minded might prefer a 'hands-off' policy in relation to the transmission of values; as such, a policy would at least avoid this charge of indoctrination (Haydon 1997).

Despite these concerns we should be very clear that it is impossible for education to be value-free. The very fact that schools exist represents a value judgement on behalf of society. Although the emphasis may change over time, values such as cultural development, knowledge, personal achievement, social justice and the need for equal opportunity underpin the whole collective enterprise of education.

Beyond their mere existence, virtually every aspect of school life is governed by values: from the choice and content of the curriculum subject to the selection of teaching methods; from classroom rules to the choices on the canteen menu. The nature of each school reflects value judgements from a range of governments, government agencies, groups and individuals. Some of these beliefs and values underlying policy will be fairly controversial. Other beliefs, such as the need for school, are almost universally accepted.[2] Either way, schools are clearly not value-free zones.

This close relationship between schools and values is reflected in the opening page of the National Curriculum: 'Education influences and reflects the values of society, and the kind of society we want to be. It is important, therefore, to recognise a broad set of common values and purposes that underpin the school curriculum and the work of schools' (QCA 1999: 10). Classrooms themselves are also value centres. If we accept the initial premise that all our actions reflect values, then the act of teaching can be no exception. 'Values are inherent in teaching. Teachers are by the nature of their profession "moral agents" who imply values by the way they address pupils and each other, the way they dress, the language they use and the effort they put into their work' (National Curriculum Council 1993: 8). For example, if one pupil publicly insulted another, the teacher would intervene. In doing so, the teacher would be promoting the values of respect and human dignity. If pupils are working on computers and one pupil insisted on having two computers for himself, denying others, then the teacher would intervene. In doing so they would clearly be promoting the values of equality and of justice in the allocation of resources. Finally, imagine that a pupil told a teacher that another boy had annoyed him and that to get his own back he was going to start a fight after school. How might we want a teacher to respond?

1   'Go for it.'
2   'Do what you feel you have to.'
3   'Why don't we all sit down and talk about it?'

Again, we would expect the teacher to promote positive values, in this case those of non-violent conflict resolution.

Teachers promote values constantly throughout the day, and this is uncontroversial. Sometimes, in all this talk of relativism, it is easy to forget that although there is wide difference in political and moral beliefs among people, there is an almost universal acceptance of certain moral values. Just because many political *beliefs* are controversial, not all moral *values* are. Indeed, some values are so ubiquitous that often we forget that they represent moral positions at all. Not hurting others, sharing resources fairly, listening, treating pupils equally, not being rude, honesty, compassion. Imagine if teachers, *en masse*, did not promote these values in the classroom; or, worse, promoted the converse of these values by encouraging violence, rudeness, dishonesty, harm, lack of compassion, unfair allocation of resources, not listening. There would rightly be public outcry!

So schools are not value-free zones and teaching involves promoting values. Further, the idea that schools and teachers might promote values is not nearly as controversial as the idea that schools and teachers might not.

VALUES AND THE CURRICULUM

So what are the values that teachers should promote? And specifically, what values should citizenship teachers promote?

Let us begin by considering teachers in general. As an NQT, you will know that in England, qualifying to become a teacher involves the evidencing of various standards set out by government. These standards also cover the professional values expected of teachers. They include the following:

> **S1.1** *They have high expectations of all pupils; respect their social, cultural, linguistic, religious and ethnic backgrounds; and are committed to raising their educational achievement.*

> **S1.2** *They treat pupils consistently, with respect and consideration, and are concerned for their development as learners.*

> **S1.3** *They demonstrate and promote the positive values, attitudes and behaviour that they expect from their pupils.*

> (TTA 2003: 7)

Key professional values of respect, consideration, concern and commitment to education are listed. Teachers are also expected to demonstrate and promote *positive values*. The exact nature of these values is made more explicit in the accompanying handbook, which in turn is derived from the National Curriculum. The National Curriculum document contains a list of commonly held values drawn up by the National Forum for Values in Education and the Community. The forum is at pains to point out that the list is by no means exhaustive nor are the values necessarily 'true'. It does however claim that the values are so widely held that: 'Schools and teachers can have confidence that there is general agreement in society upon these values. They can therefore expect the support and encouragement of society if they base their teaching . . . on these values.' The values include such elements as: 'truth, freedom, justice, human rights, the rule of law and collective effort for the common good' (QCA 1999: 195–6). The position of the document is that society holds many almost 'background' moral values which are so commonly held that teachers should promote them through their teaching. Indeed, not to promote such values would be highly unusual.

It is interesting that the forum did not wish to make the claim that these values were necessarily true. This could be interpreted as an acknowledgement that many people are relativists in relation to the truth status of moral beliefs. To claim such values as true would be controversial if many people believe that moral truth is impossible. However, perhaps such a claim is also unnecessary. Identifying a range of values as commonly held should be sufficient to suggest that they should inform teaching. Such values do not need to be presented as objectively true. The claim that they are inter-subjectively *held* as true is strong enough.

Some writers also suggest that the set of commonly held values underpins the very existence of society and shapes its particular nature. As such they can be termed 'public values' as opposed to the private values that individuals, or smaller groupings, may possess (Huddlestone 2003).

Activity 2.1   Aims, objectives and learning outcomes

Examine the list of key values in the National Curriculum document.
   Are these values you are happy to promote?
   What might promoting such values involve, both in words and actions?
   In addition to these values that all teachers should promote, are there any specific values that citizenship teachers should promote?

In conclusion, we can see that teaching is not value free and involves the promotion of key values, sometimes termed public values.

The selection and omission of the various elements of the citizenship programme of study imply various value judgements about what is important to know and what citizenship education is trying to achieve. This will be true of all subjects, but is perhaps more closely scrutinised in citizenship, as the possibility of political indoctrination is stronger. However, the wording of the programme of study itself is fairly value-neutral in its language. For example, schools are required to teach *the key characteristics of parliamentary and other forms of government*. Teaching in this area might well identify various strengths and weakness of the different forms of government. There is no suggestion that pupils ought to be taught that parliamentary democracy is the best format for governance.

Some explicit value terms do appear in the orders. At key stage 3 these are:

- the diversity of national, regional, religious and ethnic identities in the United Kingdom and the need for mutual respect and understanding;
- the electoral system and the importance of voting;
- the importance of resolving conflict fairly.

New, value-laden elements are introduced at key stage 4:

- the importance of playing an active part in democratic and electoral processes;
- the importance of a free press, and the media's role in society, including the internet, in providing information and affecting opinion.

The wording implies that it is not enough simply to teach about what a free press entails; it is also required to teach that a free press is *important*. Likewise for taking an *active* part in the democratic process, and so forth.

What emerges from this short analysis is that the citizenship programme of study is designed, in part, to reinforce the importance and value of liberal democracy. Key features of such a liberal democracy include: free-press, democratic government and freedom of religious and cultural practice.

THE CITIZENSHIP CLASSROOM

In citizenship lessons, values education takes place not only through the nature of pupil–teacher interaction, but directly through the subject matter. For many other subjects only the former is relevant. This can present an interesting challenge for the teacher. In citizenship there is clear potential for a wide disparity between what is taught (i.e., the message) and the process of teaching (i.e., the method).

We saw earlier that it is possible for a person to express one value verbally but not to behave accordingly, and there is potential for this scenario to be acted out in the citizenship classroom every day. You might prepare an excellent lesson on the importance of democratic decision making at all levels of public life. However, you might not, consciously or otherwise, carry this idea through to the pupil–teacher relationship in the classroom. The same might also be true in regard to freedom of expression. A teacher may be a passionate advocate of the principle, yet not construct the class in a way that meaningfully allows pupils to express their opinions freely. It is not difficult to imagine a teacher uttering sentences such as 'So we can see that it's vitally important for everyone to have their say . . . Put your hand down, Kylie, we'll see if there's time for questions at the end.'

Other examples where there may be discordance between form and content include:

- You might teach about the importance of active citizenship yet promote passive learning.
- You might teach about the importance of the environment yet not recycle the paper or reuse resources.

- You might teach about the importance of resolving conflict fairly yet set a whole class detention and therefore punish innocent pupils.
- You might teach about valuing diversity yet not appreciate the diversity that exists in the classroom.
- You might teach about the need to discuss our differences calmly and rationally yet not model this in the classroom, perhaps getting defensive if your views are challenged.
- You might present a one-sided lesson on issues of media bias.

If we are genuinely promoting values, then we must model them clearly ourselves. Otherwise some of the key citizenship learning points will be lost. Pupils may become disillusioned if a teacher continually talks about the struggle for democracy, yet the school does not have an effective school council and is a model of a perfect *autocracy*!

Activity 2.2

Using the list of values in the National Curriculum as well as the citizenship programme of study:

1   Highlight those that you feel strongly about, and think of ways there might be disparity between the message and the method.
2   How could the message and the methods more closely overlap on these issues?
3   Are there limits to the extent to which this can be achieved? For example, what would a fully democratic classroom be like? It is possible or even desirable?

Although it is important to marry the message and the method, it is also important to be realistic. We cannot expect teachers to model public values faultlessly at every moment of their professional lives. 'Nor do teachers have to be paragons of virtue in order to deal with SMSC [Spiritual, Moral, Social and Cultural] issues. Indeed, some of the most powerful and meaningful learning experiences occur when pupils realise that the teacher is human too' (Taylor 1998: 13).

THE TEACHER AND PERSONAL VALUES

So far we have considered values that are commonly held and should be used to inform all teaching. But this is only part of the story. What about a teacher's personal values? And what about those many issues where there is no clear consensus and a range of political and moral beliefs exists?

Dealing with personal values first, it is certainly true that a citizenship teacher's personality and interests come into the equation. The citizenship programme of study is deliberately loosely framed so as to allow for a great deal of interpretation and flexibility. In addition teachers are asked that citizenship knowledge be developed, in part, through looking at topical issues. These two features mean that citizenship teachers have a great deal of freedom in selecting and shaping the content of the subject around the lives of pupils, as well as around their own interests and expertise.

In general this is no bad thing. As long as the citizenship programme of study is adequately covered and lessons are not biased, teaching areas of personal interest should be encouraged, as it usually means teaching with knowledge and enthusiasm. However, caution should also be exercised. The freedom of the citizenship programme of study allows teachers to guide learning, quite legitimately, in many ways. But what if a teacher holds values and beliefs that are considered extreme? Perhaps they were once a member of an animal liberation group. What if they are a paid-up and highly active member of a political party? In these cases the idea of a teacher shaping the curriculum and teaching classes on certain topics becomes less publicly acceptable.

This issue is not confined to citizenship teachers. Consider the following case study.

In April 2004 a teaching story gained national media coverage. It concerned Simon Smith, a maths teacher at a Roman Catholic secondary school, who had chosen to stand for the British National Party (BNP) in the European elections.

The Local Education Authority (Solihull) decided to suspend the teacher, not citing his beliefs, but on the grounds that the press coverage had meant that his presence in schools was disruptive for pupils who were about to enter for exams. The teacher was only on a one-year contract and subsequently was not employed by the school (*Guardian* online).

Phil Edwards, BNP national spokesperson, said: "This is absolutely deplorable and amounts to unreasonable intimidation and hypocrisy. This is a good teacher who has done nothing wrong and the head teacher has made it clear she is very happy with him. This is high-level intimidation to try and stop people using the democratic process. We're no longer a free country." Another BNP member, Simon Darby, stated: "He was a maths teacher and that [position] did not give him the opportunity to bring his politics into the classroom" (Teacher TV news).

Chris Keates, NASUWT general secretary, said that police and prison service staff were banned from being members of such extremist groups, and that the same should apply to teachers. "Those who support racist and fascist agendas have no place in the teaching profession" (*Scotsman*).

Later, a DfES spokesperson added, "Schools are subject to the Race Relations Act . . . they also have the power to discipline teachers acting outside the ethos and values of the school" (*Independent* online).

This case study raises a number of questions about the relationship between teachers and values – questions that are not always easy to answer.

Activity 2.3

Using the case study above, perhaps supplemented with your own research on the case, consider the following questions:

- What different values underpin the different positions in this story?
- Should teachers be able to stand for election for any political party?
- Should citizenship teachers be able to stand for election?
- Should teachers who stand for the BNP in elections be allowed to continue teaching?
- Should teachers who are members of the BNP be allowed to continue teaching?
- Should teachers who vote for the BNP be able to teach in school?
- Would it be more pro-democracy (in the fullest sense) to allow, or not to allow, BNP candidates to teach in schools?

Some people may feel strongly that teachers should not be BNP candidates, while others may feel that as long as there is no bias in the teaching, it would be unfair not to let the teacher continue. However, as discussed earlier, values are not only promoted through the content of lessons, but through the actions and behaviour of teachers. It is clear that some of the claims of the BNP will go against some of the values outlined in the National Curriculum. By publicly standing for the party the teacher is promoting a different set of values, even if his political activities occur outside the school.

Consider a thought experiment involving a less emotive moral value – that of politeness. Imagine a teacher who in the ordinary course of life is extremely rude, but upon entering the school building adopts a set of professional values and is perfectly polite. Many people would find this to be a perfectly acceptable state of affairs, albeit not ideal. However, imagine that this teacher becomes very passionate about rudeness, to the extent that they decided to front a media campaign launched by the National Rudeness Society. Would this be acceptable?

The case study serves to show the sensitivities surrounding someone with extreme political opinions teaching in school. We might imagine the situation to be even more controversial had the individual been a citizenship teacher. This is not to say that teachers can't have political opinions or even share them with pupils. But care must obviously be taken and opinions should never stand outside the key values prescribed in the curriculum.

With the freedom of the citizenship programme of study comes the responsibility to ensure a broad curriculum and fair balance in teaching.

TEACHING CONTROVERSIAL ISSUES

Citizenship education involves far more than simply reinforcing public values. On a whole range of issues society, taken as whole, has no single voice. This is particularly true of political beliefs, although even in the realm of values there can be great divergence as to which values should be prioritised over others.[3] Every day, newspapers are filled with current affairs and debates that act out these differences, and citizenship asks that we teach about these very issues. It is inevitable that citizenship teachers will have their own opinions on many of these matters, but what should you do with your moral and political beliefs when teaching?

There are several different teaching strategies that propose answers to this question. Whatever strategy is used, though, the teacher must at all times act within the confines of the law, which can be summarised as follows:

The Education Act 1996 aims to ensure that children are not presented with only one side of political or controversial issues by their teachers. Section 406 of the Act forbids the promotion of partisan political views in the teaching of any subject in schools . . . Section 407 requires schools to take all reasonable practical steps to ensure that, where political or controversial issues are taught, pupils are offered a balanced presentation or opposing views (adapted from QCA/DfES 2001).

The key idea underpinning the legislation is that of *balance*. The act does not forbid teachers from giving opinions, but it does forbid their promotion. Promoting would be to enter a classroom with the intention of changing pupils' opinions to coincide with your own. Three of the main strategies in relation to the teaching of controversial issues are: neutral chair, balance and committed participant (QCA 1998).

Neutral chair

This involves the teacher acting as facilitator for discussion. At no stage should you present any opinions. Your interventions should be procedural (e.g., to allocate speaking rights) or educational (e.g., to clarify meanings). You may need to provide stimulus materials, however.

One key advantage of this method is that it avoids the charge of indoctrination. It has also been cited as helpful in weaning pupils away from a dependence on the teacher and encouraging the development of opinion (Bridges 1979). However, we should also note that this strategy does not necessarily produce the balance required by legislation. For example, it may produce unquestioning consensus from the entire class and it is unlikely that all of the major views will be fairly represented (Stradling *et al.* 1984).

On a more philosophical note, the very idea of neutral chair can be considered paradoxical: 'to adopt the strategy of procedural neutrality in discussion itself is to adopt, to demonstrate and quite possibly promote a specific and substantive set of values' (Bridges 1979: 124). The suggestion is that adopting the stance itself involves promoting the values of democracy, openness, commitment to reason, etc. There may also be occasions when the mask of neutrality needs to removed: for example, if a pupil makes offensive or insulting remarks, you should intervene to reduce harm and to promote public values. So the idea of being neutral is something of a misnomer.

Even when using the neutral chair method it is still possible that your opinion may unconsciously affect proceedings. Ways in which this may occur include: use of body language and facial expressions; judging the quality of argument unfairly; favouring certain speakers; preparing unbalanced stimulus materials.

Balanced approach

This might involve you presenting a range of opinions on the issue, perhaps through resource selection or by presenting different positions yourself.

One of the advantages of this method is that it is clearly in line with the legislation outlined above. Being in control of the material means that you can ensure pupils are presented with a range of opinions. Perfect balance, of course, is not realistically achievable, in part because there is no clear conception of what balance might involve. For example, in the run-up to an election should you devote equal time to examining all of the main parties, or devote time in accordance with their popularity? If the latter, what measure of popularity should you take? The status quo, opinion polls, the views of the pupils? What about minority parties? The best solution is to use common sense and make a reasonable judgement of what balance looks like in each topic.

However, having made every effort to ensure balance, you might still introduce bias by: misrepresenting the views of different parties; using unbalanced resources, solely relying on materials from a pressure group; presenting topics as binary oppositions when a range of divergent opinions exist; using pejorative or positive language – for example, *terrorists* or *freedom fighters.*

Committed participant

You make your position known, either from the outset or later, during a discussion phase.

The idea of teachers sharing their opinions on political and controversial issues is likely to cause discomfort in some quarters. The fear being that of indoctrination. Even among educationalists and academics views on this method have been divided. Some have argued that it is inappropriate: 'The inescapable authority position of the teacher in the classroom is such that his view will be given an undue emphasis and regard which will seriously limit the readiness of the students to consider other views' (Stenhouse 1970: 7) Others have said that it is the duty of the teacher to give their opinion: 'Unless the teacher comes out into the open and says in what direction he believes that the evidence points he will have failed in his duty as a teacher' (Warnock 1975: 107).

My view is that being a committed participant can be a worthwhile teaching strategy, but only in an appropriate setting. This would involve:

- Presenting opinion only in a context where pupils can both challenge your opinion and present opinions of their own.
- Ensuring that you are comfortable with your opinion being challenged and not becoming overly defensive, etc.

- Pupils being in a suitable intellectual and psychological position to feel able to question your opinion. This may mean judging pupils are age-appropriate and conducting necessary research before discussion. Naturally, the older the pupil, the more comfortable and able they will be to place the teacher's opinion within a wider framework, and so question it.
- Ensuring that overall balance is still achieved.
- Making sure you are comfortable giving your opinion. Many teachers would not want their positions on certain issues to be public knowledge, particularly in a school context. For example, a liberal teacher's position on the legalisation of cannabis may be something they would prefer to keep private.

There is no clear guidance on which of these three strategies should be used. The Crick Report suggests using common sense, and the relevant QCA guidance leaves it up to the teacher to decide, although it offers the following words of warning: 'Teachers need to decide how far they are prepared to express their own views, bearing in mind that they are in an influential position and that they have to work within the framework of the school's values' (QCA/DfES 2001: 4–6). Whichever strategy is used, one of your key aims must be to ensure that the teaching, as a whole, represents a balanced approach to the subject.

SUMMARY

The role of values in education is controversial. Two of the key controversies are: the extent to which values should be taught to pupils; and the role of the teachers' values and beliefs in the classroom. The citizenship teacher must confront both of these issues on a daily basis. This moral maze can be negotiated by being clear about the public values underpinning the curriculum and by devising suitable strategies to ensure balance is achieved.

NOTES

1 For a detailed theoretical discussion of values in relation to education, see Carr (1991).
2 Education is so universally valued that it is safeguarded in the United Nations Convention on the Rights of the Child (www.unicef.org.uk).
3 For example, at present there is debate in many Western countries about smoking in public places. This debate does not seem to be about the most effective method for achieving agreed goals but rather seems to be a question of ranking values. Nearly everyone in the world values health to some degree, and most people value personal freedom – the issue is which value should take precedence when making policy.

FURTHER READING

www.citizenshipfoundation.org.uk. The website of the Citizenship Foundation has excellent guidance on the teaching of controversial issues and also provides free teaching materials on a range of controversial topics.

Stradling, R., Noctor, M. and Baines, B. (eds) (1984) *Teaching Controversial Issues*, London: Edward Arnold. Although over twenty years old, this is still a good place to start for those wishing to explore this area in more detail.

REFERENCES

Aristotle (1988) *Nicomachean Ethics*, London: Penguin

Bridges, D. (1979) *Education, Democracy and Discussion*, Slough: NFER

Carr, D. (1991) 'Education and Values', *British Journal of Educational Studies*, Vol. 39, No. 3, pp. 244–59

Haydon, G. (1997) *Teaching about Values: A New Approach*, London: Cassell

Huddlestone, T. (2003) *Teaching Controversial Issues: Guidance for Schools*, London: Citizenship Foundation (available at www.citizenshipfoundation.org.uk)

National Curriculum Council (1993) *Spiritual and Moral Development: A Discussion Paper*, London: SCAA

QCA (1998) *Education for Citizenship and the Teaching of Democracy in Schools* [the Crick Report], London: QCA

—— (1999) *The National Curriculum: Handbook for Secondary Teachers in England*, London: QCA

QCA/DfES (2001) *Schemes of Work for Key Stage 3: Teacher's Guide*, London: QCA/DfES (QCA/01/776)

Stenhouse, L. (1970) *The Humanities Project: An Introduction*, London: Heinemann

Stradling, R., Noctor, M. annd Baines, B. (eds) (1984) *Teaching Controversial Issues*, London: Edward Arnold

Taylor, M. (1998) *Values Education and Values in Education*, London: ATL

Tomlinson, J. (1995) 'Teachers and Values: *Courage Mes Braves!*', *British Journal of Educational Studies*, Vol. 43, No. 3, pp. 305–17

TTA (2003) *Qualifying to Teach*, London: TTA

Verma, G. (ed.) (1980) *The Impact of Innovation*, Norwich: CARE Occasional Publications No. 9 UEA

Warnock, M. (1975) 'The Neutral Teacher', in M. J. Taylor (ed.), *Progress and Problems in Moral Education*, Windsor: NFER, pp. 103–12

Chapter 3   Subject knowledge in citizenship

HILARY CREMIN AND PAUL WARWICK

INTRODUCTION

This chapter deals with an area that can provoke anxiety among trainee citizenship teachers, notably the development of subject knowledge. This is because the citizenship curriculum is new, and therefore trainee teachers will not have studied it at school themselves. It is also because citizenship as a subject is so diverse (from issues of race and identity, to the EU, to sustainable development, to systems of government, to participation in the local community and so on). Very few trainees will feel qualified to degree level, or even to advanced level, in each of these disparate areas. Most teachers of citizenship, however, whether they are enthusiastic pioneers or reluctant conscripts, are unlikely to have the depth of citizenship subject knowledge that trainee citizenship teachers possess. The latter are coming into the profession with degrees in subjects like international relations, politics, communication and law. These are not degrees that would have enabled a graduate to enter teaching prior to 2001. Citizenship trainees form part of an essential workforce of specialist citizenship teachers. These specialist teachers are ground-breakers. The first step towards this pioneering role for citizenship trainees is to ensure that they are able to fill any gaps in their own existing knowledge.

This chapter will provide an overview of what constitutes citizenship subject knowledge, and what trainees can do to find out where there are gaps in their own knowledge. It will include reflections from some current and past citizenship PGCE trainee teachers. The next chapter will look at how gaps in knowledge can be filled.

This chapter aims to:

- help citizenship trainees to feel more confident about their subject knowledge;
- offer some ideas about what might constitute an acceptable level of subject knowledge for citizenship education;
- enable a process of audit and review of trainees' existing subject knowledge.

OBJECTIVES

By the end of this chapter you should know:

- that citizenship trainees have a strong starting point for the development of subject knowledge;
- what is (and is not) citizenship subject knowledge under the current English National Curriculum;
- what is an acceptable level of knowledge for a citizenship trainee teacher;
- what your own gaps in knowledge are.

You will be able to:

- carry out a process of audit and review of your existing subject knowledge and skills;
- critically review what you feel ought to be taught as part of citizenship education.

CITIZENSHIP SUBJECT KNOWLEDGE: A CONTESTED AREA

The last thing that any new learner wants to hear while developing new knowledge is 'it all depends . . .', but this is the case in citizenship education (CE). Various interest groups and different individuals have contrasting ideas about what the citizenship curriculum should look like. Due to the fact that citizenship is a new addition to the National Curriculum, it is rather vulnerable to being buffeted around as people attempt to shape it to their own pre-existing policy and practice, and it is still being confused in schools with other subjects, such as PSHE. Over the next few years, as the subject reaches maturity within the National Curriculum, and as theory and policy become embedded into practice, more general agreement about what CE is (and is not) will emerge. At this point citizenship should begin to share the benefits of other curriculum subjects, where there is a well-established body of knowledge generally accepted by the relevant professional communities.

MAPPING AND DEVELOPING SUBJECT KNOWLEDGE AS A TRAINEE CITIZENSHIP TEACHER

The rest of this chapter is devoted to activities and readings which will stimulate you to map and develop your subject knowledge. For the purposes of this chapter, I will mainly limit this discussion to what actually appears in the National Curriculum at key stages 3 and 4 for citizenship, with some consideration of a post-16 curriculum for citizenship. First, some words follow from two ex-citizenship PGCE trainees who are now teaching in schools in Leicestershire.

MEMOIRS OF SOMEONE WHO LIVED THROUGH IT!

The good news is that I am still learning about citizenship content and improving my knowledge every day, but now it's in the classroom. After accepting a place on to the Leicester University PGCE citizenship course, I received a very long summer reading list, and a list of all the subject areas I needed to be familiar with before the course began. I cried. I looked again at what turned out to be the entire *knowledge, skills and understanding* section of the citizenship programme of study; it was quickly apparent I had many weak areas. I did read newspapers (although only tabloids) and watched the news, so I had current affairs nailed. [But] the prospect of mastering the criminal justice system and the political, economic and social implications of globalisation as well as the role of the European Union, the Commonwealth and the United Nations, during one summer holiday *and* read so many books? At this point I seriously considered whether I was up to teaching, or in fact if I really wanted to be a teacher, but the commitment that got me to and through the interview drove me on.

I devised an action plan to help break up the huge task ahead. I broke down the course aims into manageable chunks, ordered the *TES*, started listening to Radio 5 (a.m. debates) and looked at the QCA website to see how citizenship was being delivered in schools. I felt some of the lessons in the QCA Scheme of Work could be made more exciting and started to look for books to help me get the information across more interestingly. The *Teacher's Toolkit* [Ginnis, P. (2002) *Teacher's Toolkit: Raise Achievement with Strategies for Every Learner*, Camarthen: Crown House Publishing] and *Thinking thorough Geography* [Leat, D. (1998) *Thinking through Geography*, Cambridge: Chris

---

Kington Publishing] gave some good examples of activities you could adapt. I also found voluntary organisations and citizenship organisation websites useful.

Citizenship is different to most National Curriculum subjects: there are facts to learn, but to have meaning for children they must always be taught in a topical context which is forever changing. Citizenship is also an active subject: children must be taught about the mechanics of the area but also have to learn about community involvement and responsible/effective participation in public life. This is tough. With thirty children of very diverse backgrounds in terms of personal opinions, how do you get them to debate without war breaking out? This is where subject knowledge is vital. If students can access facts and unbiased information, they have a good grounding to develop their own opinion. They also have to feel safe to express opinions, so creating an inclusive atmosphere in the classroom based on respect and tolerance is essential.

When you have your school experience become active yourself in the life of the school, start a debating or an interest club, join in with a school council, watch to get tips on how they are run, speak to the students about why they joined. You can have fun with school councils and really inspire children to understand what citizenship is all about. Citizenship is amazing and allows exploration of interesting concepts and ideas which you can see capture students' imagination. Many teachers and schools may not have taken the subject to heart yet, and you may feel isolated at times. Remember experience of anything new takes time, a long time; all you need to get through is enthusiasm and commitment to learning to provide the best experience for the students you teach.

Sera Shortland
Teacher of Citizenship
Hamilton Community College
Leicester

CONCERNS OVER SUBJECT KNOWLEDGE AND HOW TO OVERCOME THEM

Looking back to the start of the course, it seems so distant. It is amazing how quickly new routines, new faces and places become so familiar. In my case, the School of Education, no. 6 University Road, Leicester began as a pixel on my home computer screen, and ended as a place that I associate with friendship.

Given that the people who began the course with me were all strangers initially, it is incredible that those nine short months have led to such intense friendships. What has this got to do with the development of subject knowledge? The point is this: the fears (or at least concerns) that many of us had in relation to new challenges were overcome with comparative ease. Where they were not overcome with ease, they were generally overcome in ways that strengthened us as a group and as individuals. Prior to under-taking this course, I had numerous A levels, a degree in politics, and I had worked in the prison service for three years. Yet I was concerned about my lack of subject knowledge. Subject knowledge audits [see later in this chapter] appear to have this effect on people, and most of the 'strangers' on the course shared such concerns. We worked together to share our different areas of expertise; we shared our strengths and weaknesses and we worked together to ensure that we were all as ready as anyone can be to face the challenges of the citizenship classroom.

Jon Clarkson
Leicester PGCE, 2004–5

Next, some tasks to help you to reflect on the curriculum for CE.

Activity 3.1 Venn diagram – What I would like to teach

Take a large sheet of paper, preferably A3 or bigger, and draw a Venn diagram with two overlapping circles. The overlapping section should be quite big.

On the back of the sheet write what you would ideally like to teach, or what you think should be taught in secondary-level citizenship. Below this write what you think is in the National Curriculum at key stages 3 and 4.

Now go to the QCA website, National Curriculum Online (www.n-c.gov.uk.net), and click on 'Citizenship'. Select the programme of study (not the scheme of work) for key stages 3 and 4. Fill in any gaps on the back of the sheet.

Next turn the sheet over and write in the circles of the Venn diagram. Where the circles meet in the middle, you should write both what you want to teach and what is in the National Curriculum. To the left and the right of this, write in the circles what you want to teach (but is not in the National Curriculum) and what you do not want to teach (but is in the National Curriculum).

If possible discuss what you have written with a partner. You could consider:

- What do you think ought to be in the National Curriculum, but is not (e.g., disability studies)?
- What is in the National Curriculum that you think ought not to be there?
- What areas are you most looking forward to teaching? Why?
- What areas are you not looking forward to teaching? Why?
- Should teachers always teach what they have been asked to teach or should they have more opportunities to teach what they themselves think is important?

Hopefully there should be some agreement about what you would like to teach and what is in the National Curriculum. If there are areas that you do not want to teach because you do not know much about them, take heart! It is sometimes easier to teach something that you have only recently learned yourself. It is notoriously difficult to teach something to beginners where your own knowledge is sophisticated and complex. It is important to be able to break down everything that we teach into easily digestible, smaller parts.

Another clear way of deciding what your subject knowledge should be is to look at what your students will be examined on. As a general rule in teaching, your own knowledge should be at least one level above that of your students. That is, if you are teaching GCSE in a subject, you should ideally have A level; if you are teaching A level, you should have a degree; and so on. Although it is important that your subject knowledge goes at least one stage beyond that of your students, in citizenship teaching this may not always be possible, so this exercise is particularly useful.

Activity 3.2 Exam syllabuses

Use the blank table below as a starting point to compare and contrast the syllabi of two exam boards at GCSE level, and one exam board at Advanced level. The rows have been grouped into the areas that are covered in the National Curriculum at key stages 3 and 4, and the areas that are currently on the syllabus at Advanced level. The columns represent exam boards. Go to the websites of two exam boards, select the documentation for the GCSE citizenship course (usually downloadable as a PDF file) and then copy the areas of the syllabus into the grid. Do the same for another exam board and then for an exam board that offers citizenship at Advanced level. An example of a completed grid is shown as the Appendix at the end of this book. When you have done this, consider:

- How similar are the GCSE syllabi of the exam boards that you have chosen?
- What is distinct about each one?
- Can you see clear signs of progression at key stage 5 – post-16?
- What are the implications of this for your subject knowledge?

	GCSE syllabus 1	GCSE syllabus 2	A level syllabus
The Nature of Citizenship			
Conflict Resolution			
Community			
Culture and Race			
Business and Economics			
Human Rights			
Crime, Justice and the Law			
The Voluntary Sector			
Parliament and Democracy			
Media in Society			
Government and Public Services			
The UN and Commonwealth			
The Global Community			
Europe			
ESD (Education for Sustainable Development)			
Active Citizenship			

Activity 3.3 Subject knowledge audit

Now that you are clear about the content of what you will be expected to teach, you can audit what you already know, and where the gaps in your knowledge are, against the same areas of expertise. Use the audit tool that is shown below to begin this process of mapping your knowledge. You can use it again at various points in the year as you make progress throughout your course.

You should score yourself against the areas of subject knowledge that are set out in each row of the audit tool. Start with the pre-course (July) column and write your scores for academic study (1a–1x). personal and professional experience (2a–2x) and experience (if any) of teaching (3a–3x) in each box. Don't worry if there are gaps in your knowledge at the beginning. This is to be expected. Where appropriate, write in some ideas for action to be taken in order to ensure that you get the knowledge/experience that you need.

When you come back to this later in the year, you can give yourself a higher score in the area of academic study (1a–1x) if your independent study has led to increased knowledge that is roughly the equivalent of the qualifications named below (degree, A level, GCSE).

Academic Study (including personal study)	Personal and Professional Experience	Experience of Teaching
1a High level knowledge/skill at degree level (or equivalent)	2a Extensive experience in this area	3a Taught at A level
1b Some knowledge/skill at degree level	2b A lot of experience	3b Taught at GCSE level
1c Studied at A level	2c Some experience/informal experience	3c Taught in KS4
1d Studied at GCSE level	2d Little experience	3d Taught in KS3
1x Little knowledge/skill	2x No experience	3x Not taught

SECONDARY CITIZENSHIP SUBJECT KNOWLEDGE AUDIT

	PRE-COURSE (JULY)	OCTOBER	JANUARY	MAY
The Nature of Citizenship				
Conflict Resolution				
Community				
Culture and Race				

Activity 3.3 *continued*

Business and Economics				
Human Rights				
Crime, Justice and the Law				
The Voluntary Sector				
Parliament and Democracy				
Media in Society				
Government and Public Services				
The UN and Commonwealth				
The Global Community				
Europe				
ESD (Education for Sustainable Development)				
Active Citizenship				

The programmes of study for citizenship not only refer to students developing subject knowledge and understanding, but to these being acquired and applied when developing skills of enquiry, communication, participation and responsible action. In teaching such skills for citizenship, it is therefore important to make sure that you have these skills yourself. One person who has faced and overcome some of these issues is Paul Warwick, the deputy director of the Centre for Citizenship Studies in Education at Leicester University. He reflects here on the importance of filling gaps in citizenship skills as well as gaps in subject knowledge through his own experiences of teaching citizenship.

A PERSONAL ACCOUNT OF ENGAGING YOUNG PEOPLE IN GROUP-BASED COMMUNITY ACTION

For me, one of the exciting aspects of CE is the scope for education to move beyond the constraints of the classroom. In recent years I have worked with a cluster of secondary and post-16 education institutions on creating CE programmes that facilitate students' group-based community action. The projects that have resulted from this skills-based educational initiative have varied in focus, from students co-ordinating a food collection for a nearby homeless action centre, to another group exploring the topic of Fair Trade by creating a series of active learning activities on the topic to run in local primary schools. Creating the framework for such a CE programme has been a huge learning curve involving a continual process of mapping my subject knowledge to identify existing strengths and gaps in how best to support young people through leading community action from start to finish.

Through experience I have found one of the most effective starting points to be a consultative approach, where the participating young people are invited to consider and discuss what their concepts of community are, and where their issues of concern lie. The methods and skills for facilitating such work were initially a huge gap, and the work of people such as Jean Ruddock from Cambridge University has proved extremely useful in this area.

From this base the students on the programme are encouraged to identify a commonly shared issue, and envision possible actions that seek to make a difference. During this stage I have found it tremendously important to provide input around team-building and the development of communication skills. As the students work together on developing the design of their community action I have found another key role of the citizenship educator to be that of providing information. This role involves for example connecting with existing voluntary and community organisations in their chosen area of action, so that they can draw from others' expertise and often form partnerships and collaborative ventures.

The variety of young people's ideas for community involvement, however, necessitates extensive local knowledge of relevant service providers. I found it difficult to keep up to speed on everything, and so again this frequently felt like a personal knowledge gap. A great solution to this is networking with the local voluntary bureau or council for voluntary service, who often maintain databases of community organisations that exist locally.

With a common community action agreed upon by the students, the role of the citizenship educator then becomes that of aiding the students through the process of leading change. They are supported to work through the stages of initiation, implementation and continuation of their project. Again the mapping of my personal experiences, skills and knowledge in this area of project development and enterprise proved a vital tool for the gradual improvement and refinement of the support I was able to give. Over time I have found it useful to draw from the example of national organisations working in the area of young-person-led community action. These include Changemakers, Envision and the Get Global programme developed by the Department for International Development (DfID), along with a variety of NGOs, including Oxfam and Action Aid. Another source of support has been learning from the practice of a variety of youth service providers and informal educators such as the Weston Spirit, who work in inner-city areas within the UK.

Finally, one of my common experiences has been that young people in their novice attempts at leading community action tend to hold a determined preoccupation with the practicalities of getting their community action completed. They were sometimes resistant to taking a step back to reflect upon the process of participation, or to look at the wider political issues underlying their area of concern. A key response has therefore been to include a reflective, critical and celebratory space for such learning to take place when their action has been completed. This once again required me to look at my existing knowledge areas with regard to assessment for learning, and how to engage young people in programme evaluation effectively. The net result is that I feel that I have learned as much as my students through this skills-based CE programme, though the credit for all the amazing community actions they have been able to complete remains all theirs, and rightly so.

Activity 3.4 Audit of citizenship skills

Outlined below is an audit tool which will support you to consider the ways in which your experiences to date have contributed to your acquisition of key skills for citizenship. As before, it supports you to identify some ideas for future action to ensure that you develop the skills that you need. Use the same process as before to record your scores for academic study (1a–1x) personal and professional experience (2a–2x) and experience (if any) of teaching (3a–3x).

SKILL AREA	ABILITY	SCORE	ACTION FOR DEVELOPMENT
ICT Skills	Carry out internet-based research, taking account of different degrees of reliability and quality of information Exchange information and ideas with others using ICT Make a presentation using ICT (e.g., PowerPoint)		
Thinking/Research Skills	Review and critique multiple information sources Analyse and synthesise numeric and written information Interpret data and statistics Plan, carry out and review an enquiry or investigation Think about topical political, spiritual, moral, social and cultural issues, problems and events		

Activity 3.4 *continued*

Communicate Information	Analyse and synthesise numeric and written information Interpret data and statistics Plan, carry out and review an investigation Present findings from a project or investigation, explain results and justify methods		
Communicate Personal Opinions	Express, justify and defend personal opinions orally Express, justify and defend personal opinions in writing Contribute effectively to dialogue, discussion and debate in a group setting		
Consider Different Perspectives	Actively listen to the views of others Engage respectfully with those who may hold opposing views Explain and critically evaluate the views of others Respond to other people with imagination and empathy		
Active Citizenship (Participation at Local, National and/ or International Level)	Identify an issue of concern Explore possible responses creatively and collaboratively Create an action plan with targets, and time-scales Consider and respond to ethical and practical issues Carry out the action plan reflectively and in collaboration with others		

Activity 3.4 *continued*

	Engage in a process of evaluation and review Reflect on processes of participation		
Problem Solving	Solve problems within a group effectively Generate and compare different ways of solving problems Seek feedback and support from others, and take account of good advice		

SUMMARY

Going back to the aims and learning objectives outlined at the beginning of this chapter, it is hoped that you will now know that citizenship trainees have a strong starting point for the development of subject knowledge. You should be clearer about what is (and is not) citizenship subject knowledge under the current English National Curriculum, and what is an acceptable level of knowledge for a citizenship trainee teacher. You should be aware of your own strengths and weaknesses as a citizenship teacher, and you should have been able to identify what your own gaps in knowledge and skills are. Following on from this, you should have an action plan for developing citizenship subject knowledge and skills. Although this may appear a little daunting at first, it should be remembered that citizenship trainees are at the frontier of a new subject being implemented within schooling. A community of practice for CE is still in the early stages of being discovered. The exciting opportunity that CE trainee teachers face is the chance to help shape and form this community.

Chapter 4   Developing subject knowledge

LIZ WEST

INTRODUCTION

Subject knowledge underpins effective teaching and learning. If a teacher is deficient in subject knowledge then lesson planning, evaluation of teaching resources and activities and assessment of pupil learning are deeply flawed. Lesson planning and teaching will be poorly rooted as there is little understanding of how this lesson fits into the 'bigger picture'. A teacher cannot share with pupils how the knowledge, skills and issues explored in that lesson echo and build upon prior learning or link to future learning. At worst, there are inaccuracies in teaching which confuse and misinform pupils.

Surface understanding may lead to a heavy reliance upon the pupils' textbook without a critical reflection on its sufficiency, accuracy and 'fitness for purpose'. Inadequate subject knowledge and understanding leads to a fragile model of progression or 'what getting better at citizenship really means'. A teacher cannot effectively guide pupils forward as there is scant understanding of what progress in citizenship 'looks like'. Therefore, secure subject knowledge supports a teacher's ability to:

- Describe and explain the factual detail, themes, concepts and topical debates explored in citizenship education.
- Answer pupils' questions fully and accurately.
- Identify and correct pupils' misconceptions.
- Plan lessons that are relevant, well informed and structured to promote pupils' understanding of citizenship.
- Understand how an individual lesson fits into a wider sequence of learning and the citizenship curriculum.
- Select and use appropriate case studies which exemplify a broader theme or issue.
- Draw upon and share with pupils a range of evidence to secure rigour in discussion.
- Evaluate resources, including pupils' textbooks, media reports and relevant websites for sufficiency, accuracy and 'fitness for purpose'.
- Develop a secure model of progression within citizenship.

Developing secure subject knowledge is a continuous process, particularly in a dynamic subject such as citizenship, where the themes explored will be influenced and informed by changes within society, politics and the law.

OBJECTIVES

By the end of this chapter you should be able to:

- Identify the different elements of subject knowledge that you need in order to teach citizenship effectively.
- Identify strategies to develop and consolidate your subject knowledge.

WHAT DO YOU NEED TO KNOW TO BE AN EFFECTIVE TEACHER OF CITIZENSHIP?

Standards for Qualifying to Teach (Teacher Training Agency 2002) devotes a section to subject knowledge and understanding. The definitions include:

- They have a secure knowledge and understanding of the subject they are trained to teach.
- For key stage 3, they know and understand the relevant programmes of study.
- They are aware of the pathways for progression through the 14–19 phase in school, college and work-based settings . . . they know the progression within and from their subject and the range of qualifications to which their subject contributes.

The standards quoted above describe subject knowledge in terms of knowledge and understanding of the topics and skills named within the National Curriculum programmes of study for citizenship as well as an understanding of how citizenship 'works', for example by understanding models of progression within citizenship.

In teaching and learning, these elements are blended so that the exploration of concepts and terms is grounded in appropriate contexts and the examination of a case study will draw upon pupils' prior knowledge of the overarching themes. However, it is sometimes helpful to break down subject knowledge into manageable and distinct elements and to build understanding of these elements step by step. These elements might include:

- Substantive knowledge of each of the aspects of KSU1 within the programmes of study for citizenship at key stages 3 and 4. For example, the key characteristics of parliamentary and other forms of government (KSU1d at key stage 3). This includes: factual knowledge relating to this aspect, the specialist terms *and* substantive concepts which underpin an examination of the aspect, such as democracy, power, authority and the key debates central to this area of study.
- A sound grasp of topical debates and issues relating to the KSU1 aspects. For example: 'Is it time for a national identity card system to be introduced?' Citizenship teachers need a secure understanding of the main viewpoints held by those involved. They also need to evaluate critically the evidence used to support these viewpoints. This is essential if citizenship education is to secure an informed, deeper understanding of topical debates as stipulated in KSU2 and KSU3.
- The requirements for GCSE and post-16 options in citizenship studies: assessment objectives, examination formats and criteria for different grades. This includes coursework requirements as well as the substantive knowledge required to teach the different sections and options of the examination.
- An understanding of the main frameworks and models for the teaching and learning of citizenship within schools. This can include an understanding of how different subjects within the curriculum contribute to and inform citizenship education.

The training activities in this chapter will focus upon each of the above elements in turn. *Standards for Qualifying to Teach* notes that subject knowledge includes an understanding of progression *within* the subject. Given the specific brief of this chapter, the approach is to use the summative activity to foreground thinking about progression. However, progression within citizenship will be explored in later chapters. Some of the activities may be completed at different stages of a training course to take advantage of developments in understanding of progression that greater teaching experience can support.

DEVELOPMENT OF SUBSTANTIVE KNOWLEDGE

The first element of subject knowledge that will be examined is the substantive knowledge required to teach each of the KSU 1 aspects of the National Curriculum. One approach is to pinpoint your subject knowledge 'gaps'. These are the areas of the curriculum where your subject knowledge is insecure.

HOW DO YOU IDENTIFY YOUR SUBJECT KNOWLEDGE 'GAPS'?

An initial audit of existing subject knowledge can be a useful first step towards identifying those areas of the National Curriculum programmes of study where subject knowledge is secure and those areas that require more immediate attention. These then form individual subject knowledge training targets.

Activity 4.1

Below is one possible audit tool. It follows a three step approach.

Step 1

The first step is to use the level descriptors below to define where you are. The comments are for self-assessment purposes and define subject knowledge in terms of application to planning and teaching. Complete the first box on the grid (Figure 4.1a) that highlights prior learning and experience. Use this to decide which level best describes your existing subject knowledge of this KSU1 theme. A blank grid has been included so that you can copy out sufficient grids to audit your knowledge across all of the KSU1 themes. A worked example has also been included (Figure 4.1b). Using this overview, set short- and longer-term targets for developing your subject knowledge.

LEVEL 1

You will have studied this topic at degree level/have an in-depth knowledge due to past experience. This will be an area where you think that you have a distinctive expertise (e.g., it may have been a research focus/was central to previous experience). You could make an 'expert' contribution to a department – for example, creating a new unit of work on this topic. You will be able to identify opportunities to develop the full range of knowledge, skills and understanding and can frame meaningful, relevant and engaging enquiry questions without recourse to further reading. You can easily identify the concepts that frame rigorous examination of this theme and have a sound understanding of the main institutions, debates, topical issues and viewpoints related to this area. You will be familiar with the main protagonists/pressure groups associated with these topical debates. You could identify telling case studies which would illuminate central themes and can identify a range of ways in which pupils could demonstrate informed and

---

A Placement

Topic:				
Evidence of prior learning/experience e.g., degree/work				
Can I apply my knowledge?	1	2	3	4
Topics to be taught				
Action taken:				
Self-assessment	1	2	3	4

Targets at end of 1st placement:

B Placement

Topic:				
Action following 1st placement during 2nd HEI training phase				
Revised self-evaluation	1	2	3	4
Topics to be taught				
Action taken:				
Self-assessment	1	2	3	4

Figure 4.1a

A Placement

Topic:	The electoral system and the importance of voting			
Evidence of prior learning/experience e.g., degree/work	Overview degree module on comparison of voting systems. Experience as returning officer in student union elections (aware of strategies for secret ballots).			
Can I apply my knowledge?	1	2	3	4
Topics to be taught	KS4: 'Why bother to vote?' Is it time for the voting age to be reduced to 16? KS3: When and how do we vote? School Council campaigns – how do we run an election?			
Action taken:	Wider reading: notes and reading from: Young Citizen's Passport: Citizenship Foundation/AS Politics text. Research using materials from 'votes @16 campaign'; exploreparliament.uk; citizen21.orgschoolcouncils.org. Precis and creation of a learning activity for KS4 on BBC documentary (21/4/05). Planned sequence of learning on key questions above. Included display activity; election guideline pack for school council elections in year 8. Trained 6 pupils to act as returning officers for elections and be jointly responsible for running of election day.			
Self-assessment	1	2	3	4

B Placement

Topic:	Action following 1st placement during 2nd HEI training phase	Research on comparative systems: schools education programme.		
	Revised self-evaluation	1	2	3	4
Topics to be taught	KS3 year 9: Should voting be compulsory?			
Action taken:	Wider reading using pupils' texts/A-level texts on and using module notes from university, e.g.: Plan a sequence of lessons on arguments over compulsory voting (give specific emphasis to the development of KSU2b and KSU3a). Design an ICT webpage learning activity for pupils to propose 'Isn't it time you were heard? Increasing voting participation in school council vote campaign.'			
Self-assessment	1	2	3	4

Targets at end of 1st placement: Plan learning activity to explore different voting systems

Figure 4.1b

Activity 4.1 *continued*

responsible participation/activate their learning related to this area. You have a depth of understanding of the topic as well as being able to identify how it links to other topic areas within citizenship.

LEVEL 2

It is likely that you will have studied this topic at degree level and you feel reasonably confident in identifying the key themes, factual information debates, concepts and viewpoints central to debates. You would be able to plan relevant key questions/enquiries and can demonstrate how key concepts are explored through these enquiries. You can identify relevant case studies to illustrate the key ideas although you might need to do further research on the breadth of viewpoints involved. However, you are familiar with the main ideas and arguments used by the major pressure groups associated with the key debates. You can identify ways in which pupils could activate their learning.

LEVEL 3

You are at this level if you have a general or overview sense of the topic, but cannot independently identify relevant and specific key questions/enquiries/concepts for lessons or sequences of learning without significant further research. Lesson planning might be overly dependent on the pupils' textbook for key enquiries and substantive knowledge and you would feel unable to deal with pupils' questions that ranged beyond that general content. You have some sense of the possible case studies that could be used but are unsure of the precise issues, viewpoints central to the case study. Ideas for ensuring pupils can activate their learning are general and may not directly inform their understanding of the topic. Anything graded at Level 3 needs further work. This is likely to be a short- to medium-term target.

LEVEL 4

You should grade anything about which you know very little at Level 4. This will be a topic for which, even in general terms, you would be unable to outline key debates, enquiries or developments or deal with pupils' questions. Anything graded Level 4 will need serious and immediate attention.

Step 2

Now start to 'fill the gaps' through research and other training activities. Research should include reading appropriate texts and using media sources such as documentaries, government reports and websites of relevant organisations. Figure 4.1a allows you to frame individualised targets and to record the action taken. Review your progress and reassess your knowledge using the levels at regular intervals. For this purpose, the grid assumes a training year with two placements and two periods of HEI-based training. However, the grid could be adapted to suit your individual circumstances.

Activity 4.1 *continued*

Step 3

The third activity has been used with beginning teachers to focus subject knowledge development by applying it to a medium-term teaching plan. (See Figure 4.2a for a possible planning grid and Figure 4.2b for a *partial* worked example.) Identifying a classroom application consolidates pedagogical understanding (understanding the craft of teaching and how pupils learn about citizenship) as well as consolidating your substantive knowledge of a topic (your understanding of the main ideas, factual details and arguments). This activity can support your understanding of KSU2 and KSU3.

Choose two areas that you identified as needing urgent attention/serious work. Research into these areas and complete those sections that relate to factual details, key questions and some initial ideas for teaching and learning. You may want to complete some sections after completing some of the later activities on identifying topical issues and concepts for each KSU1 theme. It can be useful to enlarge the grid to A3 size.

Key questions	Key words/concepts	Key factual detail	Appropriate case studies/topical debates	Possible teaching and learning activities (with reference to skills of enquiry/participation)	Useful resources (teacher and pupils)

Figure 4.2a

Activity 4.1 *continued*

Key questions	Key words/concepts	Key factual detail	Appropriate case studies/topical debates	Possible teaching and learning activities (with reference to skills of enquiry/participation)	Useful resources (teacher and pupils)
What do we mean by 'voting'? Who gets to choose? Is this fair? Is it important to vote? If so, why? Why do so many people not vote?	Representation Authority Fairness Democracy Legal rights MP Parliament Election/Campaign Voter turnout	Voting rights: all citizens aged 18+ have the right to vote. NB: some exceptions (e.g., those in prison). Electoral system: a) Central government – elections at least within 5 years of start of a new government. b) UK divided into constituencies based on population – each represented by an MP. c) MP elected by 'simple' majority, i.e. 'first past the post'. NB: role of regional and national assemblies.	Is it time to lower the age qualification? If postal voting helps more people to vote, why do some argue that it is a 'danger to democracy'?	Prior learning ideas: Clips of voting on TV 'reality' programmes to lead into identification of voting and impact. Creating flow diagram on how voting works and impact. Scenario on election results and issues – to judge on fairness, security and representation (link to postal voting topical debate). Creating a campaign to encourage voting in school council election. Reflection on success and how to improve this.	For pupils: Rowe *et al.* (1998: section 5). Huddleston and Rowe (2000: section 9). Mock election resources: Hansard Society Young Citizen's Passport 2005

Figure 4.2b

An alternative activity could be to plan for teaching and learning applications through the design and use of a wall display. This should include highlighting key words and concepts (such as 'power', 'democracy') with visual representations of those terms. For example, if the theme is 'voting', you might want to link images of Parliament to images of voting. This then could link to a section of the display which outlines the topical debate over postal voting. You need to create an engaging, accessible display that highlights the essential elements of a topic.

You can increase the demands of this activity by dividing the display board into two. Target different key stages on each of the two sections. You could place the key questions and concepts/key terms in the centre of the display with arrows out to specific case studies/ learning activities geared towards the different key stages.

DEVELOPING KNOWLEDGE AND UNDERSTANDING OF KEY CONCEPTS: THE 'LANGUAGE OF CITIZENSHIP'

The second focus is conceptual knowledge and understanding. The Crick Report identified a range of concepts that underpinned and demonstrated political literacy, such as rights and responsibilities, power and authority (QCA/DfEE 1998). Political literacy requires an understanding of this 'language of citizenship' (see Douglas (2003) for an examination of how these concepts can be explored within the classroom). These concepts will be threaded throughout pupils' study of citizenship and are crucial if pupils are to understand the significance of the language used within political debate. Citizenship teachers need to have a deep understanding of these concepts and must be able to introduce 'abstract' concepts to pupils in meaningful ways. The first activity focuses on ensuring a simple working definition of all of the main concepts used within the teaching and learning of citizenship while later activities build on this to develop ways in which these concepts could be initially introduced to pupils and then developed over time so that their understanding becomes more rigorous and richer.

Activity 4.2 'Working definitions'

Step 1

This activity uses the table of concepts within the Crick Report (QCA/DfEE 1998: 44–5). Draft out a basic definition of each concept. This can act as an audit of your own knowledge of concepts. Politics and government examination texts often include a glossary. This could be a starting point for your research. You may want to add some additional terms that you think would be vital to citizenship education. (See Douglas (2003) for ideas.)

Step 2

Use the 'pairs' of concepts indicated in the Crick Report's table (QCA/DfEE 1998: 44). Identify the differences or links between the paired terms.For example: what distinguishes 'power' from 'authority'?

Step 3

Create a chart/flashcards that show the 'family' of terms linked to a concept. For example, 'Rights' could include human rights, legal rights, inalienable rights. If these cards are laminated they can be a resource for displays and teaching.

An effective citizenship teacher can introduce and explain a concept in a way that is understandable for pupils. This explanation requires an understanding of the essential elements of a concept as well as examples of the concept in practice. This initial definition is then revisited and developed throughout a sequence of learning. The following activity explores how you would introduce a concept. It can be helpful to think about the common-day usage of some terms so that you can distinguish between those terms where the common-day usage can be a starter for understanding and those where it could prove less helpful. For example, asking a pupil for the 'opposite of a right' could be met by 'It's a wrong' or 'A left'!

Activity 4.3 Introducing and contextualising concepts

Step 1

Use the medium-term plan that you started to create earlier. Complete the section on key terms and concepts on one area that needed researching.

Step 2

Identify how you will explain two of these concepts to pupils. How might you use concrete examples to demonstrate the concept? Construct and practice a three-minute explanation of a concept using one prop. For example, one beginning teacher used a Russian doll to illustrate the concept of identity, each doll signifying a 'layer' of identity, such as occupation or age. Alternatively, identify how the understanding of the concept will be explicitly linked to the teaching and learning activities. In both approaches, note down on the planning grid how you would use and introduce these two concepts.

Step 3

An extension of this activity is to plan a short learning activity which helps pupils to use the concept in context.

DEVELOPING AN UNDERSTANDING OF TOPICAL DEBATES

The National Curriculum programmes of study highlight the need for citizenship education to provide an opportunity for young people to consider and debate topical issues (QCA/ DfEE 1999: 14–15). An effective teacher of citizenship needs to be knowledgeable about such debates and the different viewpoints held. They also require secure knowledge and understanding of the underlying substantive issues and the evidence used to support the different interpretations on offer. The following activities focus upon this aspect of subject knowledge. For all of the 'topical issues' activities it is important to ground our own understanding of the issue through wider reading and research or else we fall prey to a mediated version of a debate with all of the pitfalls that this suggests.

Research should include further reading on the underpinning themes and issues so that a broader perspective is secured and a clear understanding is gained of how this topical issue fits into the 'bigger picture'. Some beginning teachers create a 'topical cuttings file' which enables them to track issues and case studies through media coverage. The file is divided under headings related to the KSU1 elements.

Activity 4.4 Case study diary

Step 1

Select an area that you identified as requiring further work. Select a case study related to this area (if you have started a topical cuttings file, you could select a case study from this). Gather together some key articles/resources/notes from TV footage using a variety of media and your own wider reading.

Step 2

Annotate these resources, bullet point the key arguments/perspectives and the evidence put forward. These annotations should highlight how it exemplifies:

- **Concepts:** 'This is an example of a conflict between individual rights and community needs.'
- **Processes:** The strategies demonstrated. For example, 'Note the use of celebrity endorsement to secure publicity.'
- **Debates:** Identify the viewpoints expressed and evaluate the evidence presented in support of this viewpoint. This is vital if you are to be able to help your pupils critically engage with evidence. For example, on the use of statistics: 'This group argues that . . . They cite . . . as evidence for this . . . However, this evidence is questionable because . . .'
- **Possible application in terms of citizenship enquiries:** Briefly pinpoint how you could use this case study for teaching and learning. For example: 'This resource is a useful individual story which would be an engaging introduction to the reasons for seeking asylum. It highlights several factors supported by the data from . . . e.g., persecution due to political activity.'

You should include any notes on recognising how to handle sensitive and controversial issues, such as acknowledging the age appropriateness of a resource or case study.

You may want to include this in the relevant section on the medium-term plan that you started in the first part of this chapter.

The above activities started to develop your subject knowledge about specific topical debates but the National Curriculum also demands that citizenship teachers support pupils' exploration of these issues through oral debate (QCA/DfEE 1999: 14–15). The following activity requires you to practise one way of modelling a presentation and marshalling of evidence in support of a viewpoint. It is a direct 'testing' of your knowledge.

Activity 4.5 Preparing a 'mini-debate'

Work with a colleague to 'model' a debate between opposing viewpoints on a topical issue.

Step 1

Identify the issue, perspectives and focus. Agree with your colleague(s) who will adopt each viewpoint. Set the date for the 'mini-debate', agree the arrangements (time allocated, prior learning for pupils). Set a date for a preliminary run-through (this is particularly important if you are a trainee teacher).

Step 2

Research the viewpoint that you are arguing. At the same time note down the challenges that you face and processes/resources you used.

Step 3

During the lesson, stage a fifteen-minute 'mini-debate' summarising your perspective and the main evidence supporting that viewpoint. Allow for questions from the floor (the class).

Step 4

Construct a step-by-step guide for pupils on how to structure and present an argument and the selection and use of supporting evidence. How would you enable pupils to do what you have done?

A variation on this approach is the 'visiting expert', which requires a depth of knowledge on a particular issue allied to a breadth of understanding over varied perspectives. In this, you act as a visiting expert on a particular issue and you handle questions from the class which can range across several perspectives. Therefore, it is a progression from the previous activity.

DEVELOPING KNOWLEDGE OF EXAMINATION REQUIREMENTS

There are several activities that can be used here. They will overlap with a growing understanding of pedagogical themes, such as assessment.

Activity 4.6 Answering questions

Step 1

Get a copy of a recent examination with the subsequent examiner's report and mark scheme. Select a small range of examination questions. Answer these questions using the time limits. Compare your answers to the mark schemes and examples of pupils' answers that are usually included in the examiner's report.

Activity 4.6 *continued*

Step 2

Using your own answers/or the examples from the examiner's report, highlight and annotate those features that you would point out as significant to pupils. For example, those features that made for effective responses. This can be enlarged and used as a teaching resource/display item.

Developing this further

Select one style of question and create a sequence of learning or a learning resource that helps pupils to tackle this style of question effectively. You can use 'shadow marking' (where you mark a sample of pupil work and then compare your assessment with that of an experienced teacher) to support your understanding of the requirements of specific sections of an examination.

DEVELOPING AN UNDERSTANDING OF CURRICULUM MODELS

Schools have adopted a variety of models for teaching and learning about citizenship. This section focuses upon developing an understanding of how different parts of the curriculum can *meaningfully* contribute to citizenship education.

Activity 4.7

Step 1

Liaise with another department and look at a scheme of learning for a year group. Identify one section that could legitimately explore citizenship themes.

Step 2

Amend that section to foreground citizenship themes, processes and debates.

Step 3

A further development to this is to place the schemes of learning for citizenship (if taught discretely) alongside a scheme from another department. Identify potential links and explicitly include these in the citizenship scheme. This should enable you to strengthen a holistic vision of citizenship education through making these links explicit to pupils. This enables your pupils to draw upon a wider frame of reference in their thinking.

One extension of this activity is to identify extra-curricular or 'learning beyond the classroom' opportunities within one year group. Some of these could have citizenship learning foregrounded within them. One challenge for citizenship teachers is to identify and make such learning explicit within their schemes of learning and within the activities so that pupils can see how all of these experiences inform their understanding of citizenship.

BUILDING AN UNDERSTANDING OF PROGRESSION INTO THE ENHANCEMENT OF SUBSTANTIVE KNOWLEDGE OF CITIZENSHIP THEMES

The summative activity in this chapter is probably best attempted after you have gained teaching experience. It brings together several elements of subject knowledge that you have been building up step by step.

As indicated earlier, part of secure subject knowledge is an understanding of progression within your subject. The National Curriculum programmes of study have elements that 'overlap' key stages 3 and 4, such as voting and the electoral system. This means that citizenship teachers must draw out more challenging enquiries and activities within and across key stages.

The following activity builds upon your earlier work and extends the planning process to include planning for progression across key stages or within a key stage. Figure 4.3 suggests one possible planning structure for this.

Activity 4.8

Step 1

Identify a key topic/KSU1 aspect and place this in the top box.

Step 2

Use the headings in each box to plan key enquiries (the questions that guide planning and teaching), key words, resources, case studies, teaching and learning methodologies for at least two year groups in key stage 3.

Step 3

Identify how these enquiries could be linked and how you could build greater challenges across the key stage. In other words, are they tackling more challenging work in year 9 than they did in year 7? This may lie in the terms introduced and used; the complexity of viewpoints examined, compared and evaluated; the types of learning chosen; and the degree of independence fostered. Some teachers use annotations along the arrows to illustrate the links to prior learning. These annotations prompt explicit references within their teaching: 'Remember when we . . .'

Step 4

If you are exploring progression across key stages, identify a further enquiry for key stage 4. Think about how this enquiry builds upon prior learning and increases the challenge from key stage 3 (look at the precise demands indicated in the KSUs). This structure can help your understanding of longer-term planning and progression within your subject.

Key topic area (KSU1)	KS3		KS3		KS4
Key enquiry/key questions					
Key factual knowledge					
Key terms/concepts					
Possible case studies (with learning purpose – i.e., 'This demonstrates . . .')					
Possible teaching and learning activities (building through KSUs 2 & 3)					
Resources					
Individual target area for planning (e.g., access and challenge/assessment)					

Figure 4.3

Subject knowledge development is likely to be a recurrent theme in your teaching career as you include new case studies, up-to-date topical debates and changes to political, legal and social structures. It is important to secure a bedrock of substantive knowledge and understanding in order to be able to reflect on the significance of debates and issues and to ensure that your pupils are able to place specific events and issues into a wider framework. In this way, they might be able to think about that event's significance. Without this foundation, citizenship education could disintegrate into a fragmented kaleidoscope of enquiries, issues and activities that may be temporarily distracting but ultimately can prove frustrating and lacks coherence. At its best, subject knowledge develops continuously, as a teacher recognises the potential and significance of resources, issues and evidence around them and wants their pupils to share in that discovery.

REFERENCES

Douglas, A. (2003) 'Educating for Change in the Political Culture?', *Teaching Citizenship*, Issue 5, Spring, pp. 8–17

Huddleston, T. and Rowe, D. (2000) *Good Thinking: Education for Citizenship and Moral Responsibility, Volume 1: Key Stage 3*. London: Citizenship Foundation/Evans Brothers

QCA/DfEE (1998) *Education for Citizenship and the Teaching of Democracy in Schools: Final Report of the Advisory Group on Citizenship* [the Crick Report]. London: DfEE/QCA

—— (1999) *Citizenship Key Stages 3–4: Programmes of Study*. London: DFEE/QCA

Rowe, D., Thorpe, T. and Graham-Maw, M. (1998) *Citizenship for All: A Wide Ability Teacher's Guide*. Cheltenham: Stanley Thornes/Citizenship Foundation

Teacher Training Agency (2002) *Standards for Qualifying to Teach*. London: TTA

FURTHER READING

Brett, P. and West, E. (2002) 'Response to Ian Davies' paper on subject knowledge', available at www.citized.info

Davies, I. (2002) 'What subject knowledge is needed to teach citizenship education and how can it be promoted? A discussion document for consideration by initial teacher education tutors', available at www.citized.info

Chapter 5   Lesson Planning

SANDIE LLEWELLIN

INTRODUCTION

This chapter provides an introduction to the process of planning for citizenship learning by bringing together guidance from available publications. Effective lesson planning involves making choices and taking decisions and can only have impact on learners when based on a full understanding of wider aims and context for teaching and learning. Good planning underpins good practice.

OBJECTIVES

By the end of this chapter you should:

- know, and be able to use, the language for planning;
- be able to link planning to the aims of citizenship;
- know how to plan to meet intended learning outcomes;
- understand the focus for citizenship lessons;
- be aware of how resources support citizenship learning;
- be able to refer to relevant health and safety regulations.

AN INTRODUCTION TO THE LANGUAGE OF PLANNING: WHAT IS PLANNING?

A plan is a method of doing something that is worked out usually in some detail before it is begun and that may be written down in some form. As adults we plan every aspect of our individual lives on a daily, weekly and longer-term basis mostly effectively, without writing things down and almost without thinking. Planning for teaching is an essential and structured activity that operates continually at a range of different levels to meet a complex set of requirements (DfES, 2002).

As Kyraciou (1998: 25) points out, planning forms one part of a wider process – it is not a stand-alone activity: 'planning is one of the three groupings that form a continuous cycle underlying the teacher's decision making'. Planning is a cyclical process that involves making decisions about how to achieve aims effectively, monitoring those decisions to identify progress, reflecting on progress and evaluating achievement to feed into future planning activities – PLAN, DO, REVIEW.

Planning for teaching needs to addresses the following questions:

- What should pupils learn?
- Why should they learn?

- When should they learn?
- Where should learning happen?
- Who should teach pupils?
- How should pupils learn?

Lesson planning is, in a sense, at the 'sharp end' of the planning process but it is important to recognise it has a distinct context. Good lesson planning is a vital part of becoming a good teacher. Many (although not all) of the difficulties encountered in teaching can be overcome by good lesson planning; however, avoid the temptation to start lesson design before you are really confident about the long-term aims for citizenship in terms of the fundamental purposes of education, societal responsibility and the specific aims of the subject.

Good planning co-ordinates long-, medium- and short-term approaches and underpins good practice; it helps to ensure teaching is focused on what pupils need to learn and make good progress, and enables staff and pupils to work together to achieve jointly agreed aims (DfEs, 2002).

STRATEGIC PLANNING

The process of planning involves constant evaluation and reflection to ensure quality and effectiveness against required national outcomes. Schools are responsible for their own self-review, target setting and improvement planning; however, in most schools where citizenship is newly established arrangements for development, modification and review may be emergent and not as rigorous as in other National Curriculum subjects. Plans to improve provision for citizenship should form part of the framework for school improvement planning. Planning at this level involves linking citizenship with initiatives across all aspects of school life.

LONG-TERM PLANNING

Long-term planning in citizenship focuses on the aims that direct activity towards broader, strategic educational and societal goals. This cannot happen in isolation. Long-term planning for citizenship happens within the context of a school's overall planned programme of work in all subjects covering every year group in a school. This is called the Curriculum Plan. The Curriculum Plan is specific to the individual school and reflects the school's context and characteristics, as well as its values, aims and priorities. The Curriculum Plan includes guidance on how the institution makes provision for citizenship and includes detailed schemes of work that specify objectives or intentions that guide the planning of units or modules of work towards achievement of the aims.

Long-term planning involves the translation of 'big picture' aims into practical plans. A focused framework of goals and objectives will allow the aims to be reached. QCA define a long-term plan as 'the planned programme of work for a subject across the school, covering one or more key stages' (www.standards.dfes.gov.uk/schemes).

A long-term plan shows how units of work in a subject are sequenced and distributed across years and key stages. Schools make decisions about the order and timing of units in a subject, focusing on curriculum continuity and progression in pupils' learning. These decisions might change from year to year to take into account new initiatives or other changes. The DfES *School Self-Evaluation Tool for Citizenship Education* (2004) offers schools a continuum to chart progress systematically using a four-stage approach and develop citizenship effectively against six areas of development. Schools should be working towards the 'Advanced' stage, with a 'a well-developed curriculum in range and depth with confident linkage of the three strands' and 'citizenship lessons are well planned for'.

MEDIUM-TERM PLANNING

This should focus on translating the aims into a framework of goals and objectives providing guidance on provision, teaching and learning steps that will allow the aim to be reached. It translates the programmes of study into coherent units of work. DfES define 'medium-term plan' as: 'a planned sequence of work for a subject (or for more than one subject) for a period of weeks, such as a half term or term, or for a number of lessons' (www.standards.dfes.gov.uk/schemes3/planning/).

When organising the three interrelated parts of the programme of study under broad headings QCA suggests three approaches that might guide the structure of the scheme of work:

- a concepts approach;
- a skills approach;
- an enquiry approach.

The concepts approach uses the key concepts identified by the Advisory Group for Education for Citizenship to provide a clear, overarching framework for citizenship that organises aspects of knowledge and understanding. The skills approach uses the development of skills required as the basis for promoting the knowledge and understanding of the programme of study. The enquiry approach uses the interests and curiosity of pupils to investigate the programme of study through the use of questions such as What? Why? How? When? Where? For example, 'Where does local government get its money from?'

Choosing one approach, or a combination of approaches, will determine how learning is achieved and will have implications for teaching styles and pupil learning outcomes.

Medium-term plans identify learning objectives and outcomes and indicate the activities that will enable these to be achieved. They usually show a sequence of activities that will promote progression and some information about the amount of time needed to cover the objectives (whether in blocked periods or regular lessons over a period of weeks).

Activity 5.1 Aims, objectives and learning outcomes

See QCA (2000: 19–22) and consider the implications for curriculum planning of the three approaches. What are the advantages/opportunities and disadvantages/issues of each approach?

	ADVANTAGES and OPPORTUNITIES	DISADVANTAGES and ISSUES
Concepts approach		
Skills approach		
Enquiry approach		

From 2001 QCA and DfES published guidance and examples of medium-term teaching and learning units in the form of non-statutory schemes of work for KS3 and KS4. The schemes of work can be found on the DfES standards site (www.standards.dfes.gov.uk/schemes) and are designed to be adapted by schools to fit in with their curriculum for citizenship. The schemes show how the citizenship programmes of study can be translated into manageable units of work.

EXAMPLE OF MEDIUM-TERM PLAN FRAMEWORK

CITIZENSHIP SCHEME OF WORK YEAR X – 20 HOURS			**Overview:** This scheme of work sets out 14 hours of lessons and 2 × 3 hour half-day sessions. The main focus is **[insert title here . . .]**		
Curriculum Requirements 1a 1b 2a etc.			*The Three Themes* **Political Literacy (PL):** **Moral Responsibility (MR):** **Community Involvement (CI):**		
Lesson Title	**Objectives**	**Learning Outcomes**	**Suggested Activities and Resources**	**Keywords**	**NC**
		ALL: MOST: SOME:	STARTER: MAIN ACTIVITY: PLENARY:		
		ALL: MOST: SOME:	STARTER: MAIN ACTIVITY: PLENARY:		

SHORT-TERM PLANNING

This focuses on implementation when small steps, or outcomes, shape progress towards the objectives for pupils. It is based on the needs of individual schools and teachers. Teachers often use short-term plans to think through the structure and content of a lesson and to note information, such as key questions, resources, differentiation and assessment opportunities, especially where this is not already included in the medium-term plan. DfES defines 'short-term plan' as 'a set of activities for a week, a day, or a lesson' (www.standards.dfes.gov.uk/ schemes3/planning/).

Short-term planning begins with units or modules from the scheme of work. These vary in the amount of detail they provide. Some schemes of work provide sufficient detail to serve as lesson plans but others are less detailed and require separate planning for each lesson. Even where learning objectives are included in the scheme of work teachers usually wish to design their own activities, choose resources to support learning and plan agreed learning outcomes and assessment opportunities with pupils. Lesson planning is an essential part of the planning process and when effective helps teachers to:

- structure lessons;
- build on previous lessons and learning;
- share the objectives of the lesson with pupils;
- assess pupils' achievements;
- develop effective assessment for learning;
- make lessons more inclusive and address a range of needs;
- make better use of classroom support;
- make explicit the key strategies they wish to use;
- address key questions they need to ask;
- highlight key vocabulary;
- focus on targets for raising standards;
- set homework (DfES, 2002).

Planning and sharing objectives with pupils has become a key principle since the introduction of the key stage 3 national strategy. It sharpens the focus on teaching and learning and so helps to raise standards by enabling pupils to make more progress in the time available. It also enables teachers to shift the emphasis from activities and what pupils *do* to what they *learn*.

CITIZENSHIP LESSON PLAN

Date	Lesson Period	Total Students	Year
Code of Practice			
Lesson Topic	**NC Context** **KS3** **KS4**		**The Citizenship Question, The Big Issue**
Lesson Objectives (WALT) **1.**			**Lesson Purpose (TIB)**

continued

Assessment Criteria (WILF)

- Students will
- Students will
- Students will

Time	Activities, organisation and pupil evidence	LEARNING OUTCOMES By the end of the lesson pupils will:
	Launch → Starter	
	Main activities	
	Extension activities	
	Plenary	
	Differentiation **All learners will** **Most learners will** **Some learners will**	
	Homework	
	Resource	

Source: PGCE Citizenship, University of Bristol (www.ole.bristol.ac.uk)

LINKING PLANNING TO THE AIMS OF CITIZENSHIP

Planning for citizenship starts with how a school interprets the two broad aims of the National Curriculum:

- to provide opportunities for all pupils to learn and achieve;
- to promote pupils' spiritual, moral, social and cultural development and prepare all pupils for the opportunities and experiences of life.

These two interdependent aims set out the values and purposes that underpin the school curriculum and provide a context within which schools plan their curriculum and all the work they do. Citizenship plays a vital role in these intentions.

The National Curriculum programmes of study for citizenship (www.nc.uk.net) set out the statutory requirement of what *all* pupils should learn through citizenship education at key stages 3 and 4. They describe the subject knowledge and content of the curriculum through three strands, and the attainment targets describe the types and range of performance that the majority of pupils should characteristically demonstrate at the end of KS3 and KS4. These, together with the three interrelated themes (social and moral responsibility, community involvement and political literacy) through which pupils develop citizenship knowledge and skills, establish the context for planning citizenship learning.

The three strands in the KS3 and KS4 programmes of study to be taught are:

- Pupils should develop knowledge and understanding about becoming informed citizens.
- Pupils should develop the skills of enquiry and communication.
- Pupils should develop skills of participation and responsible action (www.nc.uk.net).

Planning of provision should reflect the need to ensure that pupils have a clear understanding of their roles, rights and responsibilities in relation to their local, national and international communities.

Understanding the wider philosophy and aims of the subject and articulating what is trying to be achieved through the subject is important for all teachers, but for citizenship teachers it is essential if the expectations for citizenship are to be achieved. Citizenship is a complex concept that can mean different things to different people and our job as teachers of the subject is to focus on the purpose of citizenship education and how the subject relates to broader, strategic educational goals and contributes to society as a whole. Citizenship has a societal responsibility to enable the next generation of adults to embrace the values and concepts that underpin our society – freedom of speech, power with authority, equality, social justice, democracy, respect, responsibility, etc. – creating a democratic society where people matter more than things. Planning for citizenship learning needs to balance knowledge of concepts with appreciation of values and opportunities to participate in our society. If we value democracy then its continuity requires that pupils have the opportunity to develop and rehearse the skills and characteristics necessary for democratic life (www.dfes.gov.uk/citizenship). Citizenship, if it is to be effective, is more than a curriculum subject: it crosses boundaries into culture and community and this has implications for provision.

Schools have to give careful consideration to how they offer and organise their citizenship curriculum to achieve citizenship learning as there is considerable freedom. The National Curriculum does not specify how this should be done, nor is there a statutory requirement about the amount of time that should be devoted to citizenship and the balance of approaches to the three strands. QCA (2001) guidance indicates that a combination of ways might be necessary to ensure the requirements are met in a planned and systematic way and that curriculum planning must be appropriate to meet the needs of the pupils and the community. Consequently schools deliver citizenship in different ways. The following approaches are currently used:

- stand-alone citizenship lessons within the taught curriculum school timetable – the taught curriculum;
- citizenship taught through other curriculum subjects within the school timetable;
- making explicit links between aspects of citizenship and other subjects;
- citizenship taught through whole-school tutorial programmes;
- suspended timetable activities for citizenship;
- citizenship learning through wider school and community involvement.

Consider how well each of the six approaches could individually, not in combination, enable the effective delivery of the three strands of the programme of study. What would be successful and what might be overlooked? Refer to www.dfes.gov.uk/citizenship.

Activity 5.2

Stand-alone citizenship lessons within the taught curriculum school timetable – the taught curriculum	
Citizenship taught through other curriculum subjects within the school timetable	
Making explicit links between aspects of citizenship and other subjects	
Citizenship taught through whole-school tutorial programmes	
Suspended timetable activities for citizenship	
Citizenship learning through wider school and community involvement	

The curriculum structure for citizenship is a key decision in the planning process as it is likely to be a major determinant of the quality of outcomes. Decisions about curriculum provision require citizenship to be part of the regular planning cycle of review and development where regular audit starts the process. The citizenship teacher's guide (QCA 2001: 12 and Appendices 1–3) provides an audit and planning framework to help schools develop a whole-school approach to meet pupils' needs and combine appropriate modes of delivery.

Citizenship has implications for the whole school planning and therefore the ethos of the school is critical to the successful implementation of citizenship. Does the school share clear whole-school values? Are there good relationships within the school and the wider community? Do pupils participate in decision-making processes and contribute to the running of the school?

The following activity provides an opportunity to bring together the key issues that need to be considered when planning for citizenship in schools. Ofsted (2002) identified that 'best planning for citizenship began with a discussion of policy and involved governors and staff'. The activity offers the opportunity to simulate the initial stage of the policy preparation process by creating a coherent vision for school-based citizenship.

Activity 5.3 Discussion activity – our vision of citizenship

Step into each of the following roles and consider the aims of citizenship from a range of perspectives – citizenship teacher, teacher, pupils, parents, member of SMT, headteacher, governor, representatives of community groups, local councillor.
Invite each individual to contribute in turn, or 'pass', to build a group 'vision' for citizenship education by addressing the following questions:

* What might really effective citizenship look like in school?
* What would be the key features of a whole-school approach?
* How could the citizenship curriculum be planned across all key stages in school?
* What would need to change?
* What would need to be introduced?

PLANNING TO MEET LEARNING OUTCOMES

Learning objectives and learning outcomes are the small steps that enable the broad aims of citizenship to be achieved. The creativity afforded to citizenship gives generous flexibility in specifying learning objectives and outcomes. Decisions on outcomes can be decided in advance by the teacher but should increasingly be negotiated with pupils depending on their preferred learning style, strengths and weaknesses. Outcomes need to be written, clearly explained and confirmed by teachers and pupils to avoid any misunderstanding.

LEARNING OBJECTIVES

Learning objectives focus on what pupils learn as a result of the lesson and need to be developed with pupils and made explicit to pupils in a language that they can understand. The purpose of the objective is to support pupils as they move from what they know towards new knowledge, skills and understanding. Some teachers write objectives in terms of WALT – 'We are learning to . . .' others write them in terms of the expectation by the end of the lesson, for example: 'By the end of the lesson, pupils will . . .' Useful stems for learning objectives across the three strands of the programme of study for citizenship are:

Strand 1

* **know that** . . . focuses on knowledge, factual information. For example, 'There are 646 MPs in the House of Commons, elections must happen at least every five years.'
* **understand how/why** . . . focuses on understanding of concepts, effects, etc. For example, 'The concept of democracy'; 'How can we improve our environment and why should we?'

Strand 2

* **develop/be able to** . . . focuses on skills such as analysing information, applying knowledge. For example, use information on voting in the last election to explain the role of women voters.

Strand 3

* **develop/be aware of** . . . focuses on attitudes and values, sensitivity towards social issues, empathy. For example, issues and campaigns related to obesity.

LEARNING OUTCOMES

Learning outcomes are what pupils have 'learned' and can demonstrate as a result of an experience, programme or event. They are the precise stepping stones that achieve the learning objective and can be very specific ('List ten key facts about Parliament') or very broad ('Show a more positive attitude to participating in discussion'). Outcomes can be set by teachers, organisations or by the learners themselves. They can be used to assess, describe and evidence the learning that has taken place.

Some teachers find it helpful to use the WALT, TIB and WILF approach when sharing expectations.

- **WALT** is a statement of the learning objective or 'what are we learning today?' For example, we are learning about local government services, in particular whether they serve young people well enough and how you can get involved.
- **TIB** – 'this is because' – creates links with the big picture and gives meaning and relevance to learning. For example, this is because local government affects us all – we pay for and have a right to essential services and we have the power to influence the quality and quantity of them – so we should understand how.
- **WILF** – 'what I am looking for' – provides a precise statement of the learning outcome from the lesson in terms of learning, evidence and quality. For example, a clear explanation of why you feel so strongly about . . . , a list of ten services provided by local government, an action plan showing how you intend to become more involved with improving local services for young people.

The following activity is taken from the key stage 3 scheme of work (www.standards.dfes. gov.uk/schemes) and gives the opportunity to distinguish between learning objectives – what learning is intended in the lesson – and learning outcomes – evidence that the learning has taken place.

Activity 5.4 Learning objective or learning outcome?

explain the difference between civil and criminal law	understand why societies have laws
Learning Objective ❏ Learning Outcome ❏	Learning Objective ❏ Learning Outcome ❏
Why?	Why?
about the reasons for laws and the different types of law	identify the member countries of the European Union
Learning Objective ❏ Learning Outcome ❏	Learning Objective ❏ Learning Outcome ❏
Why?	Why?
the importance of debate and discussion	express your opinion and recognise the importance of respecting the views of others
Learning Objective ❏ Learning Outcome ❏	Learning Objective ❏ Learning Outcome ❏
Why?	Why?

Activity 5.4 *continued*

the most effective ways of making a difference Learning Objective ❑ Learning Outcome ❑ Why?	**describe how individuals and communities can make a difference** Learning Objective ❑ Learning Outcome ❑ Why?
summarise in one paragraph the reasons why different issues receive different amounts of media coverage Learning Objective ❑ Learning Outcome ❑ Why?	**know that there are elections at different times for various levels (local, national, global) of government** Learning Objective ❑ Learning Outcome ❑ Why?
learn about different laws that affect young people at different ages Learning Obective ❑ Learning Outcome ❑ Why?	**the different links and relations between the UK, the Commonwealth and other countries** Learning Objective ❑ Learning Outcome ❑ Why?
describe how laws are made, using examples Learning Objective ❑ Learning Outcome ❑ Why?	**list the effects of global warming mentioned on the video** Learning Objective ❑ Learning Outcome ❑ Why?
identify why people migrate from one area or country to another, recognising that some, but not all, do this out of choice Learning Objective ❑ Learning Outcome ❑ Why?	**know about the European Union and its member countries** Learning Objective ❑ Learning Outcome ❑ Why?
how the media can promote causes and campaigns Learning Objective ❑ Learning Outcome ❑ Why?	**know some of the arguments for and against membership of the European Union, for both individuals and organisations** Learning Objective ❑ Learning Outcome ❑ Why?
know how to approach and communicate with the local council and other members of the community Learning Objective ❑ Learning Outcome ❑ Why?	**know about an issue of local concern, whose interests are involved and who within the local council is responsible for dealing with the issue** Learning Objective ❑ Learning Outcome ❑ Why?

FOCUSING LESSONS

Citizenship lessons need to be R – E – A – L (Sarah Jones, South Gloucestershire LEA; www.dfes.gov.uk/citizenship).

R – Relevant

Pupils react and respond to topical, real issues that are current and actually affect people's lives; moral issues that relate to what people think is right or wrong, good or bad, important or unimportant in society; and sensitive and controversial issues that can affect people at a personal level, especially when family or friends are involved. Young people are aware of and affected by controversy. They want to talk about and understand it. Learning should be relevant to young people's experience and interests. For example, consider the responsibilities of the press by discussing the images presented in teenage magazines.

E – Engaging

Learning from real-life experience is central to citizenship education. Engaging directly with real issues and events in the life of their school or college or in the wider community gives pupils first-hand experience of citizenship in action. For example, through involvement in:

- school democracy, e.g., class and student councils;
- local democracy, e.g., youth councils, area forums;
- peer mentoring, e.g., playground buddies;
- community events, e.g., Make a Difference Day;
- campaigns, e.g., public transport, personal safety;
- regeneration projects, e.g., recycling, conservation;
- public consultations, e.g., lowering the voting age;
- planning and running charity support, e.g., Comic Relief (DfES, 2006: 108).

A – Active

Active learning is important in citizenship education because being a citizen is essentially a practical activity – it is something we 'do'. Active learning can be achieved indirectly through the use of activities based on imagined or hypothetical situations. We learn about democracy by engaging in the democratic process, how to debate by taking part in debates, and what it is to be responsible through the exercise of responsibility. Learning through discussion is important in citizenship education because it is an important vehicle for learning and a citizenship skill in its own right and gives young people a voice. It is important to recognise, however, that not all discussions are citizenship discussions. Citizenship discussions:

- are about real-life issues;
- deal with the public dimension of life;
- relate to young people as citizens (adapted from DfES, 2006: 111).

Project work is important in citizenship because it provides an opportunity for young people to take responsibility for their learning and a form of active learning. Project work can be a powerful motivator for citizenship learning. The opportunity to use initiative on an issue that concerns them can stimulate in young people a desire to find out more about how their community is run, what the barriers to change are and how these might be overcome. It also helps them to learn where they can find out these things and has a valuable role to play in the consultation process. Young people as researchers are able to provide information useful for decision-making in schools and other organisations, and in the community at large.

L – Learning

Citizenship learning is most effective when it takes place in a climate that is non-threatening, in which young people can express their opinions freely and without embarrassment and use their initiative without undue fear of failure. Such an atmosphere is built up gradually. There are a number of strategies that can help you with this, including:

- Ground rules – work best when young people are involved in developing and testing their own, e.g., for activities like discussion, or group work.
- Paired and small-group work – less threatening than facing the whole group all the time.
- Seating arrangements – to create a more open and inclusive atmosphere, e.g., sitting in a circle for discussion.
- Warm-ups and debriefs – help young people to get to know and trust each other and feel a valued part of the process.
- Giving everyone something to do – prevents individuals feeling left out and builds up a sense of group solidarity, e.g., having a vote, 'round robins', assigning different responsibilities to group members.
- Achievable goals – to create a feeling of success and avoid any unnecessary sense of failure.
- Catering for different learning styles – a range of activities employing different kinds of learning, e.g., visual, physical, written, oral.

RESOURCES TO SUPPORT LEARNING

The problem with citizenship is that there are almost too many resources, so selecting the most appropriate becomes an issue. It is essential to audit resources regularly and to develop criteria for selection to ensure resources for citizenship support the learning objectives and outcomes for all three strands of the citizenship programmes of study as a whole not just Strand 1 – knowledge and understanding. This means that in addition to websites and ICT-related resources, including video and CD-rom, texts for teachers, photocopiable resources for pupils, fiction and non-fiction, there should be recognition of the contribution of visits and visitors together with current materials in the form of newspapers, photographs and magazines. The website www.qca.org.uk/citizenship provides guidance on the effective use of people other than teachers as contributors to citizenship. Schools should work towards involving pupils in the development of criteria and the selection of resources. (See DfES, 2004 for further guidance.)

HEALTH AND SAFETY

The development of citizenship within the wider community involves planning for visitors coming into school and opportunities for pupils to make out-of-school visits. In both cases provision must meet existing health and safety legislation. *Health and Safety: Responsibilities and Powers* was sent to all schools and LEAs in December 2001. This explains who is responsible for the health and safety of school staff, pupils and others on school premises or when engaged in educational activities elsewhere, including visits. Advice on health and safety when organising educational visits can be found in the DfES 1998 good-practice guide, *Health and Safety of Pupils on Educational Visits*.

Responsibility for health and safety in schools derives from the Health and Safety at Work, etc. Act (1974) and associated regulations that place overall responsibility for health and safety with the employer. Who this is varies with the type of school. Education employers have duties to ensure, so far as is reasonably practicable:

- the health, safety and welfare of teachers and other education staff;
- the health and safety of pupils in-school and on off-site visits;

- the health and safety of visitors to schools, and volunteers involved in any school activity.

Further information can be found at: http://www.teachernet.gov.uk/wholeschool/health andsafety/visits/responsibilities/.

SUMMARY

This chapter started by with the claim that 'Planning for teaching is an essential and structured activity that operates continually at a range of different levels to meet a complex set of requirements'. Check your understanding of the context for lesson planning for citizenship by answering these two questions:

- What are the different levels of planning in citizenship and how do they interrelate?
- What requirements must be taken into account when planning an effective citizenship lesson?

REFERENCES

Department for Education and Employment/QCA (1999) *Citizenship: Key Stages 3–4*. London: DfEE.

Department for Education and Skills (2002) *Key Stage 3 National Strategy Training Materials for Foundation Subjects: Module 3*. London: DfES.

—— (2004) *School Self-Evaluation Tool for Citizenship Education*. London: DfES.

—— (2006) *Making Sense of Citizenship: A CPD Handbook*. London: DfES.

Kyriacou, C. (1998) *Essential Teaching Skills*. Cheltenham: Nelson Thornes.

Ofsted (2002) *Inspecting Citizenship 11–16 with Guidance on Self-Evaluation*, London.

QCA (n.d.) *Citizenship at Key Stages 3 and 4: Initial Guidance for Schools*. London: QCA.

—— (2001) *Citizenship: A Scheme of Work for Key Stage 3 Teacher's Guide*. London: QCA.

WEBSITES

Department for Education and Skills Standards: www.standards.dfes.gov/planning.

National Curriculum for Citizenship: www.nc.uk.net

PGCE Citizenship, University of Bristol: www.ole.bristol.ac.uk.

Chapter 6   Medium- and longer-term planning

LEE JEROME

INTRODUCTION

Medium-term plans (schemes of work, enquiries, units or projects) are crucial to providing engaging, effective and meaningful learning experiences. This chapter is primarily concerned with the process of constructing medium-term plans which effectively combine citizenship skills and knowledge in ways that promote progression and rigour. Over a period of time teachers need to differentiate through addressing a variety of learning styles; ensure pupils' understanding is developed and consolidated; and plan activities which develop pupils' skills, rather than merely reflecting prior achievement. These broad issues can only be considered across a series of lessons and so the medium-term plan provides a mechanism for focusing on these 'big' issues in citizenship and clarifying expectations about progression and assessment.

Once an effective medium-term plan is in place, individual lesson plans are much quicker and easier to write. The big questions are largely resolved, so the aims of the lesson, the links to prior and forthcoming learning, and the desired outcomes are all clear from the outset. The lesson plan then becomes useful as a mechanism for clarifying the running order and timings of the lesson, fine-tuning it to the needs and abilities of the particular class being taught and providing prompts and notes for the teacher. Put simply, starting with a well-thought-through scheme of work is likely to ease the planning and maximise the learning. On the other hand, starting the term with a great idea for an introductory lesson and a vague 'topic' to pursue is likely to create planning problems, confusion over assessment, and the lessons, while individually satisfactory, are unlikely to amount to anything more than a series of one-off experiences.

The rest of this chapter is concerned with practical approaches to thinking through medium-term plans. The ideas are developed from the author's own experience of planning educational resources and projects. Although some of the suggestions may seem rather removed from the practicalities of the classroom, they do help to establish the framework within which engaging and challenging lessons occur. The first section focuses on knowledge and understanding, and the second looks at some ideas for developing citizenship skills.

OBJECTIVES

By the end of this chapter you should be able to:

- Plan lessons in the context of medium-term planning.
- Use a range of tools and checklists to review teaching plans.
- Plan to take account of pupils' progression in knowledge and skills.

PLANNING TO DEVELOP PUPILS' KNOWLEDGE AND UNDERSTANDING

When asked to rate their own levels of confidence in relation to the programme of study, 80 per cent of teachers at key stage 3 and 60 per cent at key stage 4 say that they are confident (QCA, 2004). However, when researchers look behind these figures to consider what teachers are teaching and how they feel about it, many report concerns about almost every area of the knowledge and understanding element of the curriculum. Key areas of concern to teachers include:

- political literacy;
- central and local government;
- the legal system;
- the economy;
- Europe (Kerr *et al.*, 2004; NFER, 2004; QCA, 2004).

The lack of expertise and confidence can lead to some unexpected consequences, such as teachers claiming to have 'done' an entire area of knowledge in a single lesson (Ofsted, 2005). This clearly presents a challenge if we are to approach citizenship with the aim of pupils developing a better appreciation of the complexities of society and democracy.

In addressing knowledge teachers obviously have to be concerned with the facts about any given situation or process, and to think about how best to teach them. In a scheme of work about human rights, for example, the teacher is likely to select a number of key international agreements, such as the Universal Declaration of Human Rights and the United Nations Convention on the Rights of the Child, to provide some basic knowledge about the international frameworks that exist to define and support human rights. The teacher might also then go on to introduce some additional information about mechanisms that exist to support and defend these rights. This might include domestic legislation, such as the Human Rights Act, as well as international agencies that exist to monitor and promote human rights, such as UNICEF. Such information is important if pupils are to become informed citizens, and as they learn more they will be able to connect together bits of information to gain a better understanding of huge and complex organisations such as the United Nations. Indeed, the UN is an example of an area of knowledge which is so large and complicated that it may be better considered throughout several projects, rather than as a single, somewhat dry factual study in its own right. In this way a citizenship co-ordinator may plan across a whole key stage to cover knowledge of a particular area in the citizenship programme of study.

In addition, becoming an informed citizen involves more than just learning ever more facts about the world; it also involves developing an understanding of some deeper concepts. Being aware of this conceptual level to citizenship knowledge will enable pupils to generalise and organise the knowledge they accrue from the range of stories and case studies they encounter. A study of the law and young people may, for example, begin with an exploration of laws that directly affect pupils, as young people. At this level of knowledge and understanding they may collect and remember information about the age at which they are allowed to drive, buy alcohol, get married, fight for their country or leave school – all useful citizenship knowledge. At the same time the lessons may also be concerned with helping pupils to develop a deeper conceptual understanding of the law, social norms, the courts and Parliament. At a deeper level still, pupils may also be developing an understanding of some of the fundamental concepts that define citizenship as an area of activity. Discussions about the age of adulthood may also be used to consolidate and extend pupils' understanding of justice, fairness, rights and authority.

The precise division between each of these three levels of knowledge is less important than the conclusion for teachers that their planning must take account of the different levels of understanding of citizenship knowledge. A scheme of work about young people's rights is likely to be more effective both as a single unit of study and as a contributory element of a whole-school programme if there is clarity about what information is being taught, what specific citizenship concepts are being introduced (we might call these 'political literacy' concepts) and which basic concepts are being consolidated and extended. The following figure illustrates what this might look like in planning.

Enquiry question: Why do young people have different rights from adults?

Key content coverage	Political literacy concepts	Basic citizenship concepts
Age of adulthood in a number of different examples – laws and dates of introduction	Laws Legislation Parliament	Rights (develop from Y7) Freedom (introduce)
Court process for dealing with offences and statistics about the level of prosecutions under these laws	Courts – judiciary	Justice (introduce) Authority (develop from Y7)

Figure 6.1 Extract from year 8 scheme of work on young people and the law.

Although such a planning grid does not form a sequence of lessons in itself, it is an important first step and ensures one is clear about the potential learning for each topic before getting into more detailed planning. At this stage it is relatively easy to refine the focus and think about what needs to be developed in greater detail or with more time in the scheme of work and lesson plans that will follow.

Partly because the subject is so new and partly because citizenship is itself such a difficult term to define, there is little agreement about the precise boundaries of subject knowledge for citizenship education (Brett and West, 2003; Davies, undated). There are, however, some useful sources of information, which are considered next.

Bernard Crick has presented a number of schemas for understanding citizenship at a range of levels of generalisation. First, you might refer to the Crick Report (QCA, 1998: 44) for a list of suggested concepts that could underpin citizenship education and therefore be revisited, extended and consolidated across a range of schemes of work. These include:

- democracy and autocracy;
- co-operation and conflict;
- equality and diversity;
- fairness, justice, the rule of law, rules, law and human rights;
- freedom and order;
- individual and community;
- power and authority;
- rights and responsibilities.

In his earlier work on political literacy Crick had developed two other models which were designed to help teachers pick their way through the mass of issues, events and people in citizenship education and develop a clear vision of how to plan to revisit and extend key concepts. The 'political literacy tree' (Crick, 2003a) helps focus on the key questions teachers can use to structure schemes of work and lessons. At a more fundamental level, he has also published a proposed list of twelve primary concepts that, used in combination, provide the basis for understanding political literacy. He acknowledges that while there are more commonly used concepts, such as democracy and equality, these are always contested and the exploration of their meaning is actually dependent on an understanding of the following concepts (Figure 6.2, from Crick, 2003b):

GOVERNMENT			
Power	Force	Authority	Order
RELATIONSHIPS			
Law	Justice	Representation	Pressure
PEOPLE			
Natural and Civil Rights	Individuality	Freedom	Welfare

Figure 6.2

Of course, Crick is not suggesting that anyone should walk into a classroom and stick this diagram on the board, but he is suggesting that teachers can use such planning tools to help them clarify what is going to be most enduring about citizenship education, taken over a whole key stage. It may be that pupils study 100 or more citizenship issues, case studies or people over the course of key stage 3. How do we ensure that this all adds up to something more than 100 bits of knowledge and actually contributes to a better understanding of citizenship and political literacy? One of the ways is certainly to make sure we constantly relate the individual examples to the general concepts and perennial debates.

Anna Douglas (2003) has also proposed a useful planning mechanism for thinking at different levels of generality about developing citizenship knowledge. In her suggested planning grid (Figure 6.3) teachers are invited to plan for the following aspects of developing knowledge:

Programme of study link	Key concepts	Key questions or debates	Links to current issues	Opportunities for action

Figure 6.3

While Douglas, an experienced politics teacher, draws on her experience to extend the list of key concepts suggested in the Crick Report (Douglas, 2003: 12), Moores (2005) draws on his experience as a sociologist to think about how to explore the citizenship programme of study. He notes that many of the concepts already mentioned are common between the two subjects but also suggests that taking a sociological perspective helps us identify four themes where citizenship teachers would benefit from collaborating with sociologists:

- avoiding ethnocentric attitudes;
- understanding the importance of the nature/nurture debate;
- understanding the tension in social life between free will and determinism;
- striving for objectivity.

Fundamentally, it probably does not matter what schema you and your citizenship co-ordinator pick. The most important point is that a school's citizenship provision will be stronger if there is a strong conceptual/thematic framework that runs across the citizenship provision and enables pupils to revisit, consolidate and extend their understanding of key concepts and debates in citizenship. Without such a framework, it is likely that the whole will amount to considerably less than the sum of the parts.

Activity 6.1 Reviewing your plans

Look at the citizenship schemes of work currently in use in the school.

- Can you identify a list of key concepts that run through the school's programme?
- Is it clear when they are being introduced, when consolidated and when they are being developed?
- Is there any notion of progression evident between the treatment of such concepts across key stages 3 and 4?
- Do the schemes of work need to be revisited to clarify expectations?

Activity 6.2 Thinking about progression

The following questions are taken from a teaching resource for key stages 3 and 4 produced by Liberty, the human rights campaign group. Thinking about depth of subject knowledge only, what kinds of answers would you expect from a year 7 pupil and a year 11 pupil?

> What does the phrase 'human rights' mean?
> Where do our rights come from?
> What would you do if someone violated your rights?
>
> (Branson, 2005)

- To what extent are the differences in expectations you have written down reflected in your citizenship lessons in key stages 3 and 4?
- Try to draw up appropriate learning objectives for a year 7 lesson incorporating these questions, and then another set for a year 11 lesson.
- Do any of the citizenship concept schemas help you clarify the different expectations?
- Do all citizenship teachers in your school have a clear idea about expectations at different stages in secondary school?

PLANNING TO DEVELOP PUPILS' CITIZENSHIP SKILLS

A major civics study, completed just before the introduction of citizenship education, revealed that citizenship teachers are starting from a fairly low base, with three-quarters of fourteen-year-olds reporting that they rarely or never discussed national or international politics with their peers and two-thirds rarely or never doing so in school (Kerr, 2003). Participation is the least likely element of citizenship education to form the main focus for a whole-school programme (Kerr *et al.*, 2004). Moving towards an entitlement to participation has proved problematic for many schools, which often tend to offer *opportunities*, rather than ensuring appropriate experience (Ofsted, 2005).

On the other hand, citizenship teachers also need to bear in mind that pupils are developing transferable skills in other areas of the curriculum. In terms of discussion and debate, for example, pupils have been developing their speaking and listening skills in English, and will probably have discussed controversial issues in PSHE or RE. They will also have been developing research skills in a number of subjects, and will certainly have been taught to question sources of information through their study of history. Through the use of group work and presentations across the school, pupils will also have developed some active citizenship *competencies* (Holden and Clough, 1998) – skills which may have been developed outside the content area of citizenship, but which will certainly form the basis of any active citizenship project.

It is important to recognise the level of achievement in related subjects, for example by familiarising oneself with the relevant attainment targets across the curriculum, and also thinking about how one may help pupils make the links between their prior learning and the demands of citizenship. As with knowledge and understanding, once this prior learning is established, forward planning helps to ensure focus and progression in the development of citizenship skills.

Wales and Clarke (2005) provide a useful list of teaching activities, each of which could provide the focus for a lesson, or more likely a sequence of lessons. The following list is based on their chapter headings and forms a core set of teaching strategies:

- discussion;
- debate;
- investigations;
- role play;
- group work;
- presentations;
- simulations;
- participation in the class, year group, whole school or community.

It would be useful to take a list like this, which could be extended and refined, as a second tool kit to use at the very early stages of planning a sequence of lessons, and even as a checklist for planning across a key stage. Alongside the list of citizenship concepts, discussed above, such a checklist will help ensure skills are developed and extended and variety is maintained. Even the most interesting strategies can become tedious if used too frequently and so it is useful to think ahead about which particular strategies one should use in which contexts.

As well as planning for variety over a year or more, it is also worth building in a focus on one particular skills area in any single sequence of lessons, rather than constantly hopping from one to another. For example, allocating a few weeks to preparing for, holding and reflecting on a debate is likely to be more valuable as an opportunity to develop debating skills than simply slipping in a debate lesson in the middle of a scheme of work to liven things up a bit. While the debate itself may last only a single lesson, by considering the mechanics of how it will work, how to construct a good argument, what evidence to use, how to connect with an audience, how to work as a team to prepare a case, etc., the activity begins to link with a series of preparatory lessons. Thinking seriously about how to prepare for a debate in this manner also makes it easier to formulate a strategy for reflecting on and assessing the whole process. Pupils could be asked to assess each other in aspects of these skills, or self-assess in others, and target-set for the next time they participate in a debate, as well as reflect on the citizenship knowledge they have developed. The English Speaking Union provides advice and resources to teachers on how to plan for effective debating in schools at www.esu.org.uk. This website also includes information on competitions and training opportunities for pupils.

Activity 6.3 Planning appropriate teaching strategies

Identify a unit in your key stage 3 citizenship programme where you already have, or think you could develop, a strong skills focus through building lessons around one of these teaching strategies. Identify:

- How you (could) plan for progression within the unit, in relation to the skill.
- How this can be assessed.

While the example of debating might seem easy to plan for because it is largely classroom based, the same point can also be made for the trickier issue of participation. If citizenship teachers simply take the programme of study as the only point of reference, it seems difficult to achieve a planned and coherent series of activities across a year or key stage. And yet, the model of simply engaging in one substantial activity in three years (the minimum possible entitlement for key stage 3) also seems problematic in terms of progression and development.

The problem can only be solved by teachers thinking about how to help pupils develop the skills and competencies that can be used in subsequent community-based projects. Teachers therefore need to think flexibly about the context in which the participation takes place. Changemakers' Active Citizenship in Schools (ACiS) project takes an approach to participation which reflects this concern with progression, and their work with schools has shown that it is important to think about a series of steps towards the ultimate goal of young-people-initiated activity. They recommend teachers plan for a series of opportunities to engage with the skills of participation and responsible action through the following:

- individual activity as well as group activity (in the class or school);
- school-based activities as well as projects in the wider community;
- adult-led, young-person-centred activities, as well as young-person-led activities;
- service/helping activities as well as issue-based action.

Such a flexible model encourages teachers to accept that, while some groups of pupils are simply not ready for a fully independent, young-person-led project, nevertheless there are a number of useful and necessary steps that can be planned to build towards this final aim (Stenton, 2004). Such an approach requires careful planning and a sensitive approach to facilitating the learning so that the teacher's role does not become so intrusive that pupil participation is rendered tokenistic (Hart, 1992).

Taking such an approach to participation presents a set of issues that need to be resolved at the level of planning. Teachers without a coherent and structured programme for developing the skills of participation are likely to fail their pupils by failing to provide them with meaningful opportunities to develop their competence over time. In such a scenario, the sporadic opportunity to participate is likely to be experienced as a one-off event, with little understanding of how it can be evaluated in relation to young people's development as active citizens.

Activity 6.4 Planning for participation

Look at the units of work for citizenship over a key stage.

- How many opportunities are there for developing the skills of participation at any level and in any context?
- How are they assessed?
- Is it possible to extend any units to include relevant activities?

Activity 6.5 Pulling it all together

All of the themes and questions considered in this chapter should inform the creation of individual schemes of work. The following process may help guide you through this process, especially where you are planning for citizenship education in lessons, rather than active projects in the community. You may find it easier to involve colleagues in the planning process, at least in the initial stages, when you will benefit from the opportunity to discuss key concepts and debates.

- Identify a topic that you want to consider – this could be a specific issue or a general area of enquiry.
- Brainstorm the possible key concepts and questions that could underpin your scheme of work. You will find Figures 6.1 and 6.3 (above) useful.
- Next, think about the opportunities for developing skills and an active citizenship dimension. Do any ideas, questions or concepts suggest particular types of activities?
- You will now have too many ideas to fit into a single scheme of work and so the most important step in planning is to decide how to focus on a particular question or theme. This may be suggested by aspects of the content (for example, perhaps the idea of rights or equality emerges as a key organising principle from your brainstorm), or indeed may naturally follow a particular idea for a learning activity (for example, does the whole project appear to be best structured around a formal debate, a school-based campaign or the production of a film?).
- Once you have identified your focus for the scheme of work you should be able to plan the steps (lessons) towards the desired outcome. It is important here to consider the pupils' starting point, the knowledge and experiences they bring to the work, and the order in which issues are best encountered. Only at this stage can you begin to complete the type of planning grid that schools often use for schemes of work (Figure 6.4).

Focus/Key Question: ....

Key question(s) for each lesson	Learning objectives	Lesson activities	Resources	Outcomes/assessment opportunities
	(a) Skills			
	(b) Knowledge and Concepts			

Figure 6.4 Scheme of work

SUMMARY

Planning is necessary to ensure progression and clarity in teaching. Without some notion of how teaching and learning build on prior experience and attainment, and an idea of how it will be extended in the future, it is more difficult to make sense of individual lessons. If medium-term plans include the level of detail discussed in this chapter, the lesson plan itself becomes much easier to write as the focus and purpose of the lesson is clear from the outset. Such an approach to planning will also help to rectify some of the initial problems observed with the implementation of citizenship and help to make citizenship learning more rigorous and challenging.

REFERENCES

Branson, S. (2005) *A Teaching Pack for Citizenship at Key Stages 3 and 4*, available at: www.liberty-human-rights.org.uk/resources/education-pack/pdf/teaching-pack.pdf [accessed 24/04/05]

Brett, P. and West, L. (2003) *Subject Knowledge and Citizenship Education*, available at: www.citized.info/pdf/commarticles/PB_LW_citizenship_subject_knowledge.doc [accessed 24/04/05]

Crick, B. (2003a) 'The Political Literacy Tree', *Teaching Citizenship*, 5: 18–22

—— (2003b) 'Back to Basics', *Teaching Citizenship*, 7: 24–9

Davies, I. (undated) *All Teachers Need Subject Knowledge*, available at: www.citized.info/pdf/commarticles/Ian_Davies2.html [accessed 24/04/05]

Douglas, A. (2003) 'Educating for Change in the Political Culture?', *Teaching Citizenship*, 5: 8–16

Hart, R. (1992) *Children's Participation: From Tokenism to Citizenship*, Innocenti Essays No. 4, Florence: UNICEF International Child Development Centre

Holden, C. and Clough, N. (eds) (1998) *Children as Citizens: Education for Participation*, London: Jessica Kingsley

Kerr, D. (2003) 'Developing Effective Citizenship Education in England: Using the IEA Civics Education Study to Inform Policy, Practice and Research, symposium paper presented at AERA conference, Chicago, 21–5 April

Kerr, D. *et al.* (2004) *Citizenship Education Longitudinal Study Second Annual Report: First Longitudinal Survey – Making Citizenship Education Real*, Research Report 531, Slough: NFER

Moores, M. (2005) 'Sociology and Citizenship', *Social Science Teacher*, 34, 2: 12–15

NFER (2004) *National Evaluation of Post-16 Citizenship Development Projects: Key Recommendations and Findings from the Second Year of Development*, Brief No. RB507, Slough: NFER

Ofsted (2005) *Citizenship in Secondary Schools: Evidence from Ofsted Inspections (2003/04)*, London: Ofsted

QCA (1998) *Education for Citizenship and the Teaching of Democracy in Schools: Final Report of the Advisory Group on Citizenship* [the Crick Report], London: QCA

—— (2004) *Citizenship: 2003/04 Annual Report on Curriculum and Assessment*, London: QCA (QCA/04/1491)

Stenton, S. (2004) 'Community Action and Young Person Led Participation', in B. Linsley and L. Rayment (eds), *Beyond the Classroom: Exploring Active Citizenship in 11–16 Education*, London: New Politics Network

Wales, J. and Clarke, P. (2005) *Learning Citizenship: Practical Teaching Strategies for Secondary Schools*, London: RoutledgeFalmer

Chapter 7 Planning, evaluating and auditing the whole-school provision

RALPH LEIGHTON

INTRODUCTION

> In the majority of schools much or all of citizenship has been placed within PSHE programmes . . . [but] the perceived close relationship between citizenship and PSHE is proving problematic. Taking the broad view, PSHE is about the private, individual dimension of pupils' development, whereas citizenship concerns the public dimension . . . Often, schools claim the content of lessons is citizenship when it is in fact PSHE.
>
> (David Bell, Her Majesty's Chief Inspector of Schools, 2005)

The place and nature of any citizenship programme must be set in the context of the school's aims, culture, ethos and values. Citizenship education is not only about lesson content, and not all schools teach citizenship as a specific subject. Whether the intention is to maintain subject provision or to develop and enhance it, the first step in planning and evaluating whole-school provision must be to conduct an audit which will clarify the current situation. This will enable the school to ensure that time and other resources are used to best effect, that statutory requirements are being met, and that repetition is avoided.

As more citizenship departments are established, it is likely that many new or relatively inexperienced teachers will take on responsibility for the planning and auditing of citizenship. An audit of the curriculum, however citizenship is delivered, will enable subsequent strategies and developments to be planned and implemented in a rational and effective manner. Once you know which aspects pupils have already met, you will also know which can be built upon and which have to be introduced as new. An effective and accurate audit also enables you to consider what must be delivered specifically as citizenship and therefore what must be involved in planning units and separate lessons.

Evaluating the effectiveness of provision depends largely upon the effects which are desired. If your intention is to address as much of the National Curriculum as possible, 'effectiveness' will be measured against criteria different from those which apply if the intention is to enable pupils to become active, informed and responsible citizens. It may be that, in successfully addressing one target, you also manage to meet the other. This chapter is intended to enable teachers of citizenship, whether new or experienced, to meet those twin objectives.

OBJECTIVES

By the end of this chapter you should be able to:

- identify the extent of citizenship provision in your school, understanding what has been done so far and what has still to be done;

- incorporate awareness of pupils' own knowledge and experiences into your planning and teaching;
- plan units of work which will enable pupils and the school to develop;
- evaluate the effectiveness of citizenship provision and consider ways of increasing that effectiveness.

AUDITING CITIZENSHIP PROVISION IN YOUR SCHOOL – MAPPING WHETHER THE CURRICULUM IS BROAD AND BALANCED

There are many different timetable structures and many different ways of organising the delivery of citizenship in schools (Cleaver *et al*. 2003; Leighton 2004a; Bell 2005). Add to this the fact that schools are encouraged to tailor their provision of citizenship education to meet local circumstances, and it becomes apparent that auditing and mapping the citizenship curriculum is a crucial and exacting strategy. If aspects of citizenship are being delivered through other subjects or activities, it is important to avoid repetition and to ensure that time and resources are used to full effect.

At the same time, it is not enough simply to identify subject or topic headings; it is also necessary to ensure that the citizenship characteristics of a topic are identified and addressed. For example, aspects of mass media might appropriately feature in the key stage 3 curriculum in English and modern foreign languages, but both would approach it from a perspective specifically relevant to those subjects rather than from an agenda explicitly informed by citizenship. Subjects have their own character and content, and all of the National Curriculum has to be delivered by schools. Bell (2005) offers an important reminder that the cross-curricular nature of citizenship provision can be problematic. The best way to gain a clear idea of how the subject is being addressed in any context is to conduct a detailed initial audit as outlined in Activity 7.1. In order to clarify which areas are not being addressed (thereby not meeting National Curriculum requirements), and those which are being duplicated (thereby creating unnecessary pressures on staff and pupil time), as well as those which might appear to be meeting some of the statutory requirements, the first step in identifying what needs to be done for the citizenship curriculum must be to discover in detail what is already in place.

This should be done with a view to what is appropriate to each school's context. It is not possible to deliver the whole citizenship curriculum in equal depth and detail, nor is this required. It is also necessary to keep in mind that citizenship is concerned with skills as well as knowledge, and that planning might focus on an ideal but success may depend upon being able to bring colleagues, pupils, parents and others along. Be prepared to identify and build in opportunities for others to support and contribute to the development of citizenship provision.

Activity 7.1

1 Use a reliable and proven system to audit your school, for example the DfES's *School Self-Evaluation Tool for Citizenship Education* (Lloyd *et al*. 2004). This will take quite some time, but it is an investment which will pay dividends by giving a clear picture of what is provided and what is needed.

2 From the data gathered, list the key attitudes, concepts, knowledge and skills of citizenship education being taught and learned in your school, within which subjects and how they are being taught and learned, and also list those which are not yet being taught and learned.

3 Think about how the differences between the two lists might be addressed and resolved. It is the second list – what needs to be done – which should become the focus of planning and evaluation.

Activity 7.1 *continued*

4   Extension activities:

    (a) On the basis of 1, 2 and 3, above, identify both what a comprehensive citizenship policy for your school should include and what changes would be required in order to implement that policy.

    (b) On the basis of (a), above, and the other tasks in this chapter, write the policy.

BUILDING ON AND TAKING ACCOUNT OF PUPILS' PRIOR EXPERIENCE AND KNOWLEDGE

Although citizenship might still be considered a new subject – in some schools it remains a subject in waiting – a lot of the content is not wholly new. It has been regularly pointed out (for example, Crick 1998; Ross 2003) that citizenship education builds on activities which many schools have regarded as essential for some time and could in the past have been 'seen in work pupils were already doing in the community, in contributions pupils made to the running of the school or simply in the way that what children learnt in the classroom related to what was going on outside the school gate' (Bell 2005).

Once you have completed the audit of the school curriculum you can begin planning as you will now have a clear idea of what is being done and what still needs to be addressed. If you have found that a good quantity and quality of citizenship education is already present, it is important to build on this for pupils to develop their understanding, knowledge and skills; even if there was not a substantial amount overtly covered prior to the systematic introduction of citizenship, it is likely that you will have found some aspects of the curriculum which have been addressed through other subjects. If neither of these situations applies, you might find that your pupils have other experiences and knowledge – from youth associations, young people's media, personal and peer experiences – through which citizenship education can be introduced to them or through which their interest and awareness can be developed and sustained.

Building relevance and recognition into subject delivery to create or enhance a sense of continuity is not something which happens only within key stages or within particular phases of education. As Claire and Holden (2004) show, much of the good practice in key stage 2 can be lost in the early stages of key stage 3; this period of transition is full of new experiences for pupils and it may be that, by linking primary experiences to the secondary curriculum, we can enable them to settle more quickly and effectively as well as enabling them to make progress within the subject.

Activity 7.2 will enable you to find out with which aspects of the National Curriculum your pupils have some familiarity and therefore where their prior experiences and knowledge lie. You will also find areas of consensus and of disparity, which, given that year 7 pupils may have come from a variety of schools with very different approaches to education in general and citizenship in particular, will enable you to identify and work on common ground as well as differentiating materials according to identified needs. The nature of the activities – card sort, negotiation, presentation, discussion, peer assessment, voting – will also indicate the extent of pupils' familiarity with some of the subject-specific skills of communication and participation identified in the National Curriculum.

Activity 7.2

- Organise a class into groups of five or six.
- Give each group a set of cards, each one representing one of the knowledge areas for the appropriate key stage of the National Curriculum (DfES 1999).
- Each group should select three topics and produce a brief outline to the class on why they regard them as important. They should also be given the opportunity to outline and advocate a topic not in the set of cards.
- The class can then negotiate between groups, through discussion and voting, which five topics they regard as most important.
- Keep the outcomes of the above activities with your audit and policy produced in Activity 7.1 so that the issues, knowledge and skills raised and identified can be properly addressed in your planning.

PLANNING A UNIT OF WORK

When Bell (2005) wrote that 'citizenship is the worst taught subject at Key Stages 3 and 4', he was commenting as much on poor planning and lesson structure as on content. Even when lessons are seen to be satisfactory or better, these are often single lessons or approaches unique to particular teachers rather than part of a cohesive departmental approach (Leighton 2004a). When planning a unit of work, it is essential that you have the outcomes of Activities 7.1 and 7.2 in mind, if not to hand. Each lesson should fit with others to make a cohesive unit, and each unit should fit with others to create a coherent course, within a clear set of values and a whole-school ethos.

While the debate about assessment in and of citizenship is far from resolved, there are many opportunities for assessment in citizenship, and a variety of purposes to which the processes and data can be put. Jerome (2004) clearly indicates that assessment strategies have to be considered at the outset of planning in order to make it useful and effective; he also, very usefully, provides considerable insight and advice on how to approach assessment planning. Other issues to be borne in mind include all cross-curricular and national strategy focuses, teaching and learning styles, as well as ensuring that the full range of skills and knowledge is addressed across the units as a whole rather than necessarily within each one.

Since there is no uniform structure to school days or timetables, as well as little consistency in the amount of time given to various subjects, it is not possible here to give a specific structure to units of work. These must be tailored to the time and resources made available by each school, although it must be stated that schools which do not provide time, staffing and other resources adequately will find it very difficult to meet their statutory obligations with regard to citizenship provision.

The template in Figure 7.1 implies six sessions for a unit; it may that timetabled sessions are fifty minutes a week in some schools, an hour a fortnight in others, and some of yet different duration and frequency elsewhere. There is nothing to say that all units have to be of equal length, as what constitutes 'appropriate' duration can depend upon many factors. All units should address the full range of learning styles and provide a number of learning activities, keeping the National Curriculum requirements clearly in focus. There should also be an element of flexibility so that lessons can be interchanged, allowing pupils and staff access to resources. With the increasingly frequent use of 'focus days' or 'collapsed timetables', consideration should also be given to how these can enhance citizenship provision, and how they can be used better to address specific aspects of subject skills and/or knowledge.

The following activity should enable you to match classroom work and other strategies to National Curriculum topics. As well as finding that there may be a number of ways to

Session	Learning objectives	Intended outcomes	Resources	Areas	Assessment	Literacy	Use of ICT	Numeracy	Active citizenship	Cross-curricular links
1.										
2.										
3.										
4.										
5.										
6.										

Figure 7.1 Unit planning template

address particular issues, it will give an overview of strategies so that a series of units can be developed within which there is not too much repetition, yet pupils can develop skills and familiarity in relation to particular learning activities.

Activity 7.3

- Consider the list of activities and strategies below:

Class discussion	Instruction	Research exercise
Cross-curricular activity	Lecture	Showing a video
Focus day	Literature search	Simulation
Focused questions	Observation	Statistical data
Group discussion	Off-site activity	Team teaching
Hot seating	Open questions	Textbook focus
ICT	Outside speaker	Video conferencing
Independent learning	Problem solving	Working in silence

Identify four activities which would enable effective learning in each of the following areas: controversial issues; mass media; social and cultural diversity.

- Take any one of the areas identified and develop the activities to ensure that they enable National Curriculum requirements to be met.
- Looking back at Activity 7.1, points 3 and 4, identify which elements of your school's provision have now been addressed.
- Continue with 1–4 in relation to all aspects of the citizenship National Curriculum.

EVALUATING THE EFFECTIVENESS OF THE CITIZENSHIP CURRICULUM

The extent to which citizenship provision is successful depends upon the criteria for success. Some schools may be satisfied with meeting the statutory requirements to the letter while others clearly aim to espouse a spirit and ethos of citizenship beyond curricular demands. For some, citizenship is a subject while for others it is an attitude. This dichotomy makes it necessary that there is an understanding of the desired effect before steps are taken to evaluate the effectiveness of provision.

For those schools where the expectation is to meet the requirements of the National Curriculum, attention must be paid to the skills as well as the knowledge requirements. In situations where the intention is to go further than statutory obligations, to create an atmosphere and ethos compatible with the principles of citizenship, evaluation may have to be deeper. In both cases it will have to be carried out over a reasonable time span and, crucially, be regularly repeated.

One way in which it is possible to verify whether objectives have been achieved is to reconsider those objectives. Activity 7.1 required that you identify what needs to be done in your school; if the outcome of that activity was accurate and your response complete, you will know that the objectives are met by checking actions and outcomes against the lists which completion of the activity produced. If outcomes are uneven, you have a picture of where more needs to be done and some idea of what it is that is lacking.

For those schools that wish to see their pupils become positive and active members of society, it would be appropriate to refer to the local community to investigate the extent to which this has happened. In the same way as Activity 7.2 is consciously focused upon the perceptions of young people, the second task in Activity 7.4 is based on an awareness of the need to work with local communities. Through the dynamic programme of study, and other planned activities which comprise citizenship provision, you should have developed practical and positive links with local organisations and individuals; their opinions and perceptions could be invaluable to recognising the success of your programme so far, and to offering advice and support for its future development.

Activity 7.4

- Identify three local agencies with which you have worked on delivering citizenship – e.g., a local NGO, community police officers, faith groups – and ask for their perceptions of the school community. Next year, ask them again. Whenever the school works with outside agencies, ask for perceptions and opinions. These need not be taken at face value, but can be considered and reflected upon.
- Ask teaching and support staff for their perceptions of the effects of the citizenship programme. Ask pupils. Ask those with domestic or caring responsibility for the pupils. Remember that you are not asking how to adapt or improve the citizenship programme but trying to build up a long-term picture of its effects. Again, individual responses need not be taken at face value, but can be considered and reflected upon.
- Re-do Activity 7.1, having completed the other activities and implemented their outcomes. If you get the same results, you need to re-do the activities.

SUMMARY

Not only is the nature of citizenship education and the content of the National Curriculum likely to change over time, but the nature and content of other subjects is likely to change. Therefore, the relationship between all subjects needs to be regularly assessed and evaluated in order to ensure development and balance throughout the curriculum. It follows, then, that each of the activities in this chapter should be regularly – if not frequently – revisited. This will serve to keep policies up to date, enable content to remain relevant to pupils' changing experiences, ensure that planning is always fresh and appropriate, and provide a curriculum which is tailored to the needs of the school.

REFERENCES

Bell, D. (2005) 'Speech to the Hansard Society', available at: http://www.ofsted.gov.uk/

Claire, H. and Holden, C. (2004) 'Effective Transition KS2–KS3', available at: http://www.citized.info/

Cleaver, E., Ireland, E. and Kerr, D. (2003) 'The Citizenship Education Longitudinal Study', *Teaching Citizenship*, 7: 15–19

Crick, B. (1998) *Education for Citizenship and the teaching of Democracy in Schools: Final Report of the Advisory Group on Citizenship*, London: QCA

DfES (1999) *Citizenship: The National Curriculum for England*, London: DfES/QCA

Jerome, L. (2004) 'Planning Assessment for Citizenship Education', available at: http://www.citized.info/

Leighton, R. (2004a) 'The Nature of Citizenship Education Provision: An Initial Study', *Curriculum Journal*, Vol. 15, 2: 161–81

—— (2004b) 'Trainees, Mentors and Citizenship: Fair Conflict Resolution Begins Here', *Teaching Citizenship*, 9: 26–31

Lloyd, J., Kerr, D. and Newton, J. (DfES Citizenship Team) (2004) *The School Self-Evaluation Tool for Citizenship Education*, London: DfES

Ofsted (2003) *Inspecting Citizenship 11–16 with Guidance on Self-Evaluation*, London: HMSO

Roland-Levy, C. and Ross, A. (eds) (2003) *Political Learning and Citizenship in Europe*, Stoke-on-Trent: Trentham

Ross, A. (2003) 'Children's Political Learning: Concept-Based Approaches versus Issue-Based Approaches' in C. Roland-Levy and A. Ross (eds), *Political Learning and Citizenship in Europe*, Stoke-on-Trent: Trentham, pp. 17–33

WEBSITES

http://www.citized.info/
http://www.dfes.gov.uk/citizenship/
http://www.ofsted.gov.uk/
http://www.standards.dfes.gov.uk/schemes2/citizenship/?view=get
http://www.qca.org.uk/schemes
http://www.teachingcitizenship.org.uk/

Chapter 8   Assessment in citizenship

MARY RICHARDSON

INTRODUCTION

Effective assessment practice will contribute to improving standards and achievement in citizenship (QCA, 2002), but it has been suggested that assessment might be more difficult to measure in subjects such as citizenship than in other curriculum subjects (Lyesight-Jones, 1998). Effective assessment is rooted in getting the right information from pupils in the most efficient way and it should be an integral part of your teaching and learning programme for citizenship.

OBJECTIVES

By the end of this chapter, the reader should have:

- developed a knowledge of planning the assessment of citizenship;
- recognised a range of learning styles and should be able to identify means of differentiation;
- developed an understanding of common learning problems and ways to tackle them;
- recognised some of the issues related to assessment of citizenship education.

ASSESSMENT OF CITIZENSHIP

There is a wide range of assessments available for citizenship, and the setting of clear expectations together with the involvement of pupils in the assessment process will promote motivation and help pupils to engage with citizenship. But what is meant by 'assessment'?

Assessment is an overarching term which, when applied in the classroom, might include some or all the following:

- written tests and examinations;
- portfolios;
- practical examinations;
- oral presentations and examinations;
- coursework;
- teacher observations;
- self-assessment;
- peer-assessment.

Teachers have been required to assess pupils' attainment in citizenship at the end of key stage 3 since August 2003. The end of key stage description (see www.qca.org.uk) divides evidence of pupil attainment into three categories: knowledge, skills and participation. Pupils are required to:

1. demonstrate a broad knowledge and understanding of the topical events they study; the rights, responsibilities and duties of citizens; the role of the voluntary sector; forms of government; provision of public services; and the criminal and legal systems;
2. show understanding of how the public gets information; how opinion is formed and expressed, including through the media; and show how and why changes take place in society;
3. take part in school and community-based activities, demonstrating personal and group responsibility in their attitudes to themselves and others.

(www.qca.org.uk)

Assessing the knowledge outlined in category 1 is reasonably straightforward: pupils' knowledge can be demonstrated through written tests, coursework and presentations. However, assessment of the skills required for categories 2 and 3 is more challenging and requires some thought to be given to what might be appropriate for pupils. Although there are no statutory arrangements for assessment at key stage 4, some qualifications, including short-course General Certificates in Secondary Education (GCSE) in citizenship studies, are offered by three English awarding bodies. Essentially, it is up to you to decide upon the most appropriate way of assessing progress and rewarding achievement for pupils at the end of key stage 4. If you decide to offer a qualification such as a GCSE at key stage 4, then consider all of the specifications available and talk to the staff responsible for citizenship at the awarding bodies to find out what further resources are available to support and develop your teaching. Awarding bodies can provide a range of support, including INSET training, recommended textbooks and specimen examination papers. Awarding bodies currently offering a GCSE short course in citizenship are listed at the end of this chapter.

Citizenship education presents both the pupil and the teacher with many different contexts in which assessment can take place (Kerr, 2002). Just as you might adopt different approaches to the teaching of citizenship, there is a variety of ways in which pupils' progress can be recorded and their achievements recognised and celebrated. When planning assessment of citizenship, you might consider presenting pupils with some of the following as ways of recording progress:

*   a diary or logbook;
*   evidence of participation in a school event, e.g., a video recording of proceedings;
*   a talk supported by an OHP or a PowerPoint presentation;
*   the development of an educational game or a website;
*   evidence of communication with an MP or a local councillor;
*   literature about an organisation and a written account of voluntary work with that organisation;
*   worksheets.

Citizenship is unusual and exciting in that the approaches to assessment are necessarily flexible. Therefore, you should consider which types of assessment will motivate and inspire your pupils to optimise their achievements in citizenship. Successful implementation of assessment is grounded in the knowledge that you have about your pupils as learners. The following sections will allow you to identify ways to ensure you can help your pupils learn more effectively and take responsibility for the development of their education in citizenship.

LEARNING STYLES AND DIFFERENTIATION

Learning styles

We all favour particular styles of learning, and identification of suitable assessments can be facilitated if you have some knowledge about the learning styles of your pupils.

Figure 8.1 is adapted from the learning styles summary designed by Honey and Mumford (2005). It is possible to identify four types of learner – activist, pragmatist, reflector and theorist – and, as Figure 8.1 shows, describe the optimum learning characteristics for each.

Think about your own learning style. You will probably find that you identify with more than one style and most of your pupils will also demonstrate a combination of learning styles. Therefore, it is important to know which are their strongest and which require development. Use the next activity to help identify the learning styles of your pupils.

ACTIVISTS	**PRAGMATISTS**
Activists like to be involved, to get stuck in and demonstrate enthusiasm for new ideas, but they can easily become bored. They tend to have a 'ready, fire, aim' approach and although they work well in teams, they can dominate group tasks.	Pragmatists are keen to try new things, are practical and bring a no-nonsense approach to their work. They engage well when learning about concepts that are directly related to the task in hand, but can be impatient with lengthy discussions.
Optimum learning opportunities for the activist	*Optimum learning opportunities for the pragmatist*
• Any new experiences, particularly problem-solving • Team tasks, including role-playing and leading • Being 'thrown in at the deep end'	• Any task that is clearly linked to an end result • Techniques with obvious advantages, e.g., saving time • Use of a clear model which they can copy
Pupils who are activists dislike listening to long explanations and are less confident when working alone. They prefer not to follow instructions to the letter and like to take action immediately.	Pupils who are pragmatists are less interested in learning when there is no obvious or immediate benefit that they can recognise or if the task has no clear guidelines.
REFLECTORS	**THEORISTS**
Reflectors will consider a situation from many different perspectives. They are systematic and like to consider findings before deciding upon conclusions. They like to observe others and enjoy discussing results.	Theorists tackle problems in a methodical manner and tend to be perfectionists who like to compartmentalise their learning. Theorists can be detached and/or analytical rather than subjective or emotive in their thinking.
Optimum learning opportunities for the reflector	*Optimum learning opportunities for the theorist*
• Observing individuals, groups or situations • Reviewing information or situations to consider what has happened and what has been learned • Generating analyses and reports	• Complex learning situations using existing skills and knowledge • Structured situations with a clear purpose • Consideration of ideas/concepts which might not be immediately useful/relevant
Pupils who are reflectors prefer not to lead and are not always confident about presenting work in front of their peers. They like plenty of time to consider and prepare tasks and can be put off when thrown in at the deep end.	Pupils who are theorists do not usually enjoy participating in situations which emphasise emotion and feelings or when they feel they are out of tune with the other participants, e.g., working with pupils of opposing learning styles.

Figure 8.1 Learning styles

> ### Activity 8.1
>
> Draw up a learning descriptor grid (based on Figure 8.1) and title each square with a learning style. Place each of the pupils in your class within the framework based on their strongest learning skills. Think about a project that you are going to present to the class to work on in groups and consider how you might group pupils most effectively based upon their learning styles.

Differentiation

Differentiation is a term that is often used to describe the process teachers go through to make lessons accessible for pupils with learning difficulties (Jerome, 2004). However, it is important to understand that differentiation is integral to your programmes of teaching and learning. You might not organise your citizenship classes by ability, but you need to develop a thorough knowledge of each pupil's abilities in order to provide an appropriate learning experience for all. Jerome (2004) classifies differentiation into six categories; a condensed version is presented in Table 8.1, below.

Table 8.1 Approaches to differentiation

Differentiation by	Method
Content/resources	Pupils work on a similar theme, but with a variety of resources. You may decide to provide everyone in the class with all resources, or direct specific resources to specific pupils.
Activity or task Organisation	Pupils have the same resources to use, but work on different questions or tasks. Pupils work in mixed-ability groups and on other occasions pupils are grouped by ability; or Pupils work in pairs, thus encouraging a culture of peer support.
Support	You might spend more time with more able students in one lesson and then focus on those experiencing difficulties in another lesson. You may enlist the help of a teaching assistant.
Gradation/extension	Pupils work with the same resources, but questions become more difficult as the lesson continues; or Pupils start the lesson with a common activity and the addition of 'extension' work moves pupils on at a different pace or level.
Response/outcome	Pupils preparing for a citizenship GCSE get used to working on open-ended questions and producing an individual response that can be levelled. Careful planning may help you set common tasks with common resources, but it is likely that teaching (as opposed to assessment) will also draw on one of the previous strategies.

Activity 8.2 Aims, objectives and learning outcomes

Using Table 8.1, identify the differing needs of the pupils in your class and consider how you plan to address them. Select one stimulus source, for example a newspaper article, and construct a lesson plan which presents tasks appropriate to pupils' differing learning needs; encourage pupils to work alone and then in small groups to discuss their opinions and responses.

COMMON MISUNDERSTANDINGS ABOUT CITIZENSHIP

This section lists some of the common misunderstandings about the assessment of citizenship and suggests ways to address them. It is likely that you will encounter many misconceptions about citizenship while teaching the subject, but rather than view this as a problem, keep a collection of the most common, or your 'favourites', to use in lessons as starting points for discussions.

A mark is the measure of a citizen

It is important that pupils, parents and others understand that the assessment of citizenship is not a test of 'goodness of the individual'. Some assessments review pupils' knowledge: for example, pupils might answer a written examination comprising questions about the electoral system, or they might present a portfolio related to voluntary work for evaluation. While it is possible to assess and grade both of these types of evidence from pupils studying citizenship, the final mark awarded for the work is not a reflection of citizenship ability.

Activity 8.3

Discuss the different modes of assessment available with your pupils to ensure that they understand how their work in citizenship will be evaluated. Divide the class into groups and assign each a mode of assessment; they must research and present this assessment and argue its case by explaining why and when it will be useful.

For example, one group could present a video of a school council meeting and argue that this demonstrates active participation; another group might present a sample examination paper (downloaded from an awarding body website) and discuss the value of the qualification; and a third group can explain that marks in citizenship describe their achievement in the subject and are not a reflection of the individual.

We know what citizenship is . . .

Everyone has an opinion about citizenship education. The problem is that everyone has a different opinion. Some might say, 'That's the class about being good, isn't it?' while others might ask, 'Is it something to do with voting?' Citizenship is part of busy school curriculum so pupils need to understand where and when it is being taught, particularly when it is taught using a cross-curricular approach rather than as a discrete lesson. Pupils also need to understand that the assessment of citizenship is something that, unlike many other subjects, involves them being proactive about the recording and review of their progress.

Ensure that pupils are clear about what comprises their citizenship education. Ask them to identify learning for citizenship in different situations, for example in a classroom, at home, within a community setting or at a whole-school event.

Citizenship is the same as PSHE

Although the dominant model for citizenship has been that of PSHE, it is a very different subject. Research from Ofsted has shown that many schools still treat the two subjects as one. It is important that the status of citizenship is clear and the subject is valued in its own right. Present students with some key concepts and learning outcomes for both citizenship and PSHE. Ask them to compare and contrast the two.

KNOWING WHERE PUPILS STAND

At the start of each lesson or project, pupils should be made aware of the goals and outcomes for learning. If this practice is established from the outset, there is less chance that students will misunderstand what is expected of them. As mentioned earlier, citizenship affords pupils the rather unique opportunity to take more responsibility for managing the recording and review of their own learning. However, for reporting purposes, you need to know where they stand. Use Figure 8.2 as a means of working through the process to see where each pupil is.

With reference to the QCA guidance on assessment of citizenship (QCA, 2002), Table 8.2 develops further questions to use when recording your pupils' progress.

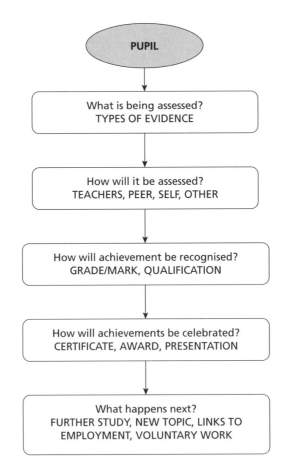

Figure 8.2 Pupil achievements

Table 8.2 Recording progress

Task	Question
Identify assessment partners	Do you/your pupil know what type of assessment will be used? When, and with whom, will pupils use peer assessment? How will pupils manage self-assessment? Who else might be involved in assessment of their progress?
Establish expectations	Are pupils clear about what is expected for each lesson, for each project, by the end of term? If pupils are working towards a formal qualification, are they clear about the learning outcomes? How is this information presented to pupils? Do you have any exemplars of work to which pupils can refer?
Agreeing targets	How will goals be set and achieved? How often will progress be discussed? Are pupils clear about their responsibilities for self-assessment and peer assessment? Do pupils know the dates of examinations? How will pupils deal with issues which might affect progress towards goals?
Reporting and reviewing evidence	How will evidence of learning be selected? How will assessment of the evidence be documented? Have you drawn up a timetable for discussing assessments with individual pupils? What evidence might be submitted towards a qualification (e.g., for GCSE coursework)? How will achievements be reported to parents?
Rewarding achievements	Is there an opportunity to report to the whole school? Have you made use of the local media to highlight a successful school–community project? Is there a prize-giving or similar presentation day where achievements in citizenship are recognised? Have you made a note of the date that exam results are published? How might successful group work be rewarded?
Continued review	What have you learned from the last lesson/project, term, etc.? Are there subjects or topics that merit further investigation? Did you identify problems/issues and consider how they might be dealt with in the future? Did you identify any personal skills or knowledge that might benefit from further development?

PARTICULAR ISSUES RELATED TO ASSESSMENT OF CITIZENSHIP EDUCATION

Like all subjects, citizenship has its idiosyncrasies. The following are just some of the issues that are particular to citizenship. As with the misconceptions, it is useful to keep your own records of issues in order to consider how you can address them effectively within your school.

- Assessment of subjects through cross-curricular routes is difficult. Ensure that you know where and when citizenship learning is taking place so that it is possible to identify learning outcomes that can be recorded and included in pupils' records.
- Official guidance emphasises the idea that assessment should be creative and varied, thus evidence of attainment can include a range of media, for example video, verbal presentations, computer-based work as well as written work. However, you need to

understand that a wide variety of approaches to assessment might not always be realistic. It is important to select and promote methods of recording work for assessment that are manageable within the context of your framework of teaching.

- Make use of all the support that is available when planning and developing assessments. Get in touch with the citizenship team at QCA. If you decide to offer a GCSE (or other qualifications), talk to the citizenship subject staff at the awarding body; they can inform you about additional information and training that are available.
- Evidence of learning should be of a high standard. Schools need to develop approaches of recording attainment in citizenship that encourage pupils to produce and collate work that is of an equal standard to that in other subjects.
- Offering a formal qualification such as a short-course GCSE has been shown to benefit standards in some schools. Research from Ofsted (2005) found that pupils' achievements and standards were often higher when students were working towards a recognised qualification.

SUMMARY

To some extent, the development of a clear model of progression in citizenship still hinders the development of assessment. It remains difficult to be precise about what it means to achieve in citizenship. Just as pupils play an integral part in the learning of citizenship, it is teachers who will assist in the development of models of good practice. The flexible delivery and assessment of citizenship can be used successfully to support the different learning styles of individual pupils. Choosing a variety of approaches to assessment can improve pupil motivation and affords pupils a tangible sense of achievement in citizenship.

SOURCES OF INFORMATION

Citizenship curriculum and assessments

Department of Education and Skills (Citizenship Team) – www.dfes.org.uk/citizenship
Qualifications and Curriculum Authority (Citizenship Team) – www.qca.org.uk
National Curriculum Online – www.nc.uk.net
Nuffield Curriculum Centre – www.nuffieldcurriculumcentre.org

Awarding bodies (offering a citizenship qualification)

Assessment and Qualifications Alliance – www.aqa.org.uk
Edexcel – www.edexcel.org.uk
Oxford, Cambridge and RSA – www.ocr.org.uk

Support and ideas for teaching

Citized – www.citized.info (Teaching resources and information for trainee teachers)
Citizenship Foundation – www.citfou.org.uk (Provides information, resources and covers all aspects of citizenship education)
Association for Citizenship Teaching – www.teachingcitizenship.org.uk (For case studies, teaching resources and lesson plans)
Institute for Citizenship – www.citizen.org.uk (Works with teachers and students to form effective models of citizenship education)

REFERENCES

Campbell, J. (2000) 'Assessing Citizenship: Opportunities and Challenges', *Citizenship Update* (Autumn), No. 3

Honey, P. and Mumford, A. (2005) 'Learning Styles', available at: <http://www.campaign-for-learning.org.uk/aboutyourlearning/whatlearning.htm>

Jerome, L. (2004) 'A Briefing Paper for Trainee Teachers. Citizenship Education and Pupils with Learning Difficulties', available at: <http://www.citized.info>

Kerr, D. (2002) 'Assessment and Evaluation in Citizenship Education', paper presented at British Council seminar, Beijing, July

Lyesight-Jones, P. (1998) 'Assessment Issues within Personal and Social Development', in S. Inman, M. Buck and H. Burke (eds), *Assessing Personal and Social Development: Measuring the Unmeasurable?* London: Falmer Press

Ofsted (2005) *Citizenship in Secondary Schools: Evidence from Ofsted Inspections (2003/4)*, London: HMSO (HMI 2335)

Qualifications and Curriculum Authority (2001) *Citizenship: A Scheme of Work for Key Stage 3 – Teacher's Guide*, London: QCA

—— (2002) *Citizenship at Key Stages 1–4: Guidance on Assessment Recording and Reporting*, London: QCA

Chapter 9   Leading citizenship

DARIUS JACKSON AND RUSSELL MANNING

INTRODUCTION

Citizenship is a new subject in schools and is having a troubled childhood (Ofsted 2005). Even Libby Purves commented on the difficulties citizenship was having in schools (*Education Programme*, BBC Radio 4, 17 May 2005). Ofsted make it clear that poor decision-making is one of the biggest factors in citizenship's poor report this year (Ofsted 2005). So if it is going to prosper it needs effective leadership of the subject in schools.

OBJECTIVES

By the end of this chapter you should:

- be able to develop strategies to raise the status of citizenship in your school.
- be developing strategies to market citizenship to parents and your colleagues.
- have highlighted strengths and concerns within the teaching of citizenship in your school.
- be confident with a number of strategies useful in handling the headteacher, members of the SMT and colleagues.
- have analysed a case study in raising the status of citizenship.

LEADING CITIZENSHIP

The importance of leadership is central to a discussion of school improvement (see Barker 2005 for a discussion of this). The need for the support of the headteacher cannot be overstated for the development of citizenship: 'There can be no effective whole school strategy for Citizenship evaluation without the full support of the Head and Senior Management Team' (Potter 2002: 120). This 'effective . . . support' will help to prevent the poor decision-making derided by Ofsted.

Placing middle managers at the centre of the consideration of school leadership is a relatively new idea. Traditionally, in discussion of school leadership, the central role was given to headteachers (Brundrett and Terrell 2004: 7). However, in recent years emphasis has shifted and the concept of leadership has been broadened to include middle managers (Bennett 1999: 289). Admittedly, though, there is some discussion as to whether they are 'leaders' or just 'managers'. This is because subject leaders have an ambiguous position. Are they primarily downward conduits for leadership decisions or upward conduits representing their departmental interests? Do they make school policy or merely make sure it is implemented? This ambiguity leads to the regular complaint that being a head of department means 'everyone is free to kick you!'

To help understand this complex situation, Busher and Harris (1999: 307–8), based on work by Glover, argue that heads of department have four 'dimensions' to their job:

- '. . . transactional leadership role' where they use their authority to secure agreement by colleagues to carry out policies. These policies may be at school or department level;
- '. . . foster collegiality . . .' by developing shared visions within the department;
- 'supervisory role' in monitoring pupil performance and supporting colleagues' performances;
- 'representative' of the department to outside agencies and senior managers.

In this chapter we shall focus on a number of these roles as we consider how to go beyond mere survival in schools. We need to study a number of things. How does a middle manager champion citizenship within the school and beyond. How can you co-opt the headteacher as an ally? And where do you find support?

As we consider other issues and a case study, we hope to show that middle management in school is about, above all else, transformation: 'How do we move this subject along?' This is in terms of its success and status within the school, and in terms of its internal cohesion; the degree to which all of the teachers agree with and implement departmental practice. To enable you to prioritise areas, it is useful to develop an overview of where citizenship is starting. DfES's School Evaluation Tool for Citizenship Education (available from www.dfes.gov.uk/citizenship) provides a good starting place. From this you should be able to produce a development plan for citizenship.

RAISING STATUS IN SCHOOLS (OR KEEPING THE HEAD HAPPY)

Activity 9.1 Why is subject status important?

Think about the schools in which you have worked. Which subjects had high status? What benefits did this status bring these subjects?

Busher and Harris (1999) explain that status comes from a number of factors, most of which are amenable to change. This first one, alas, is not. Some subjects traditionally have higher status: mathematics, science and English are all heavyweights; they dominate the school curriculum and resources. Other subjects need to work hard to gain and maintain their status.

Luckily, there are other factors which are within our control: 'The status a department acquires depends upon the academic and technical performance of the students it teaches, on its contribution to the extra-curricular activities of a school and on the quality of the profile it helps the school to gain within its local community' (Busher and Harris 1999: 313). Acquiring status for the department is essential as it is an effective means to acquire 'extra resources'. Consequently, any citizenship co-ordinator must keep the headteacher up to speed with the subject and work with other subject leaders who are sympathetic.

Activity 9.2 How many times in the last two weeks have you discussed the state of citizenship with the following?

	Formally	Informally
Headteacher		
Deputy/assistant head		
Other head of subject		

It is impossible to overemphasise the importance of good contacts with your headteacher. Headteachers are busy people. Consequently, if you 'drop in' for an informal chat it is a good idea to know exactly what you want them to have learned from you at the end of the conversation. From our experience of running departments (a little over thirteen years between the two of us) headteachers respond best to solutions and success. They need to know their subject leaders both solve problems and raise the school's profile.

Where schools have a rigid hierarchy you will need to keep your line manager informed as well as opening up lines of communication directly to the head. The next area to consider is how should a new head of department communicate with other subject leaders?

HORIZONTAL COMMUNICATION

'Networking . . . is endemic to organisations. It is quite useful for middle managers in secondary school to share information, ideas and concerns' (Fleming 2000: 17).

Activity 9.3   How do subject leaders see each other?

Think about the school you work in.

- Which subject leaders have status within the management? These are people whom other subject leaders consider to be the big hitters.
- Which subject leaders are not big hitters?
- Which subject leaders are seen as 'awkward customers'?

You will need to use different styles of communication; an informal chat with the head is completely different from an agenda-based meeting with your line manager. You also need to work out which other subject leaders can help you plan the delivery of citizenship. This is not just in terms of subject matter – RE studying diverse beliefs; geography studying world trade and poverty – but also attitude:

- Which ones do you find it easy to work with?
- Which of them is amenable to an advance from citizenship?
- Which of them can carry their team with them?
- Which department is the most innovative?

COMMUNICATING WITH THE CITIZENSHIP TEAM

This is probably the most important part of a subject leader's job – communicating with and building a subject team. Obviously it is going to be easier in subjects with clearly defined boundaries and a high degree of pedagogic cohesion. Citizenship, as a new subject, is trying to define the boundaries and pedagogies (Jackson 2005; Davies, Harber and Yamashita 2005).

The other problem you are likely to meet is the make-up of your team. Many schools have put citizenship into another area, subject or time slot. Consequently, it can often blur into PSHE, or may be taught by all teachers in tutorial time. These strategies are not helping citizenship develop its borders and practices, and this contributes to the poor state of citizenship in schools. In a recent Ofsted report (Ofsted 2005), one in four schools had citizenship provision defined as 'unsatisfactory'. Where citizenship is working, it is taught either by a small team of subject specialists or a 'significant partner' in PSHE. The shared features are that 'citizenship has sufficient time, an identity to which pupils can relate and building blocks which together establish coherence and progression' (Ofsted 2005: 4). Developing this 'coherence and progression' must be the target for citizenship co-ordinators. Clearly the curriculum time issue is to be negotiated with the headteacher; so how are you going to build a team to give citizenship its identity?

On ITT courses time is spent considering how to motivate a range of pupils. Running a team of teachers is similar; it is all about motivation. There is a series of rules of thumb:

- **Consult**. Teachers love to discuss their ideas and are happy if their leader consults.
- **Take time**. Do not try to change everything at once: plan changes over a number of years and communicate the plan to the whole team. Make time to talk to your team.
- **Charm**. Anyone who is less supportive needs to be brought on board. Take time to canvass their ideas and discuss contentious issues with them.
- **Praise** loudly and honestly.
- **Share good practice and ideas**. Use an agenda item to make teachers share their ideas.
- **Mistakes**. We all make them, so don't make a fuss, just pick up the pieces and smile.
- **Make decisions** when they are needed. Do so openly and explain your choice.

The qualities of a good team have been around for a long time, Brundrett and Terrell (2004: 85) list twenty. These are worth considering:

Shared values and beliefs	A focus on learning and learners	Leadership from different people on different tasks	Having clear departmental policies and procedures . . .	Having policies that are developed from school policies . . .
Moral purpose	Engagement in the department	Good inter-personal relationships	Positive humour	A sense of direction
Sharing	Collaboration	Co-operation	Enquiry	Reflection
Evaluation	Criticality	Involvement	Vision	A sense of achievement

Activity 9.4 Strengths and areas to improve

From Brundrett and Terrell's list, select four that you are good at and four you need to work on. Then decide what you are going to do to improve. This can be done as a team.

Where citizenship is taught by the whole staff you need to go beyond a small team to manage a range of teachers, some of whom will be at least indifferent and possibly even hostile to the subject. Though the comments by Hannam, Smyth and Stephenson (1976: 167) are not new, they are valid: 'There is nothing simple about becoming a member of an established staff group and the newcomer needs to develop an awareness of its structure and methods of communication. Most will learn haphazardly or through trial and error.' You need to understand the informal structures in the staffroom and use them to help develop your subject. Staffrooms are hotbeds of politics and a young subject leader needs to aware of this. You must be conscious that citizenship is a controversial subject. With a commitment to active learning, participation and children's rights, it challenges the ideas that children are the recipients of education and above all else need to be controlled. Teachers have deep-seated ideas about pedagogy that stem from their personal philosophical stances, so your new ideas will inevitably unsettle a few of your colleagues. This is also nothing new. Back in the 1960s Morrison and McIntyre (1969) described not only how young teachers became less progressive as they established themselves in school, but also how conflicts between teachers were often about expectations of pupil behaviour. As in running a department, the trick is to decide who will support you and who will oppose your ideas, and to respond accordingly. You will never be able to develop citizenship if you are seen as a staffroom cynic. However, if you can convince the other teachers it is not a bad idea, you will have defused a problem early.

MARKETING CITIZENSHIP

Marketing schools and subjects is inevitable. Teachers are often unhappy about this, but it is part of the job (Oplatka, Hemsley-Brown and Foskett 2002). As is shown above, a subject leader is always engaged in marketing: trying to convince the head of geography that a link-up is a good idea, convincing the head that GCSE (short-course) citizenship for all is a winner or stressing that the history department teaching about the suffragettes is not quite enough. It's all marketing!

Before we consider marketing, it is crucial to remember that the best way to market any subject is through the quality of teaching. If the pupils arrive expecting an exciting, dynamic lesson in which they can express their ideas they will tell everyone how excellent citizenship is. That is why team building is central to running a department.

The three most important areas for you to market citizenship are to the headteacher, to the parents and to the wider community.

The headteacher

In their report on citizenship, Ofsted (2005: 3) said that where teaching of citizenship is poor, 'key management decisions were based on misunderstanding or scepticism'. Consequently, your head needs to know:

- How you are planning to develop the subject, why these areas are a priority and what the timescale is.
- How citizenship will raise the profile of the school in the local community.
- How citizenship will help raise the standard of education in the school.
- How you will raise levels of collegiality in the school.

Parents

This is about more than convincing parents that citizenship is a worthwhile subject. Research by Cathie Holden (2004: 257) concluded that 'parents were largely ignorant of what was going on in schools with regard to citizenship education but held clear views about this area of the curriculum and wanted to know more'. So ask yourself, will parents see:

- A convincing and passionate rationale for citizenship teaching in the school?
- A clearly thought-out programme of lessons, which shows the lessons are exciting and thought-provoking?
- Evidence to show pupil progress in citizenship?
- Reporting which is clear and precise?
- That the subject has high status in the school by the prominence it is given in the prospectus and in displays?

The wider community

Marketing to the local community is all about looking for opportunities and seizing them.

- Which local organisations are involved in citizenship work?
- Which political parties are willing to come into school and which are good at inspiring the pupils about politics?
- Which local issues impact upon your school?
- Which charities enable us to participate rather than simply raise money?
- Are there any local groups set up to support teaching citizenship?
- Does the local university teach citizenship; if so, at what level and how can we join in?

OTHER AREAS OF SUPPORT

The obvious place to look for support is among the advanced skills teachers of citizenship. These people are employed to support the development of citizenship in schools. They have a wealth of ideas and enthusiasm.

There is also the Association of Citizenship Teachers, which produces an excellent journal and organises conferences. (See www.teachingcitizenship.org.uk.)

The CitizEd website (www.citized.info) is similarly full of ideas. Even though this is intended for trainee teachers, you will visit it time after time as it includes plans, discussions and articles.

Don't forget the QCA (www.qca.org.uk), DfES (www.dfes.gov.uk) and Ofsted (www.ofsted.gov.uk) websites. There is plenty of useful material on all of them. *Inspecting Citizenship 11–16* from Ofsted is very good as a tool for self-evaluation of teaching and learning in citizenship.

Any consideration of charities and pressure groups is quickly outdated and doomed to be partial, but there are some we would recommend as we use them on the PGCE course:

- Amnesty International (www.amnesty.org.uk)
- Citizenship Foundation (www.citfou.org.uk)
- European Parliament (www.europarl.eu.int)
- Holocaust Education Trust (www.het.org.uk)
- Institute for Citizenship (www.citizen.org.uk)
- Let's Kick Racism out of Football (www.kickitout.org.uk)
- Teachers in Development Education (www.tidec.org)
- Unicef (www.unicef.org.uk)

For a more exhaustive list of websites, see Appendix Three in Gearon (2003).

CASE STUDY: PROMOTING CITIZENSHIP THROUGH A HOLOCAUST MEMORIAL DAY

I [Russell Manning] taught history for ten years in a comprehensive school in Dudley. In 2002 I travelled to a neighbouring school and had the privilege of listening to an Auschwitz survivor talk about his wartime experiences. The pupils and teachers who heard these recollections were inevitably moved. This encounter brought history to life and engendered a feeling of empathy for those who had to endure such terrible suffering. After witnessing the success of this day I decided to arrange a similar event at my school for the whole of year 9.

At the time I was a teacher of history, not a head of department, and had no responsibility for promoting citizenship. Below is a description of the procedure I went through in order to organise this event.

Getting the 'go ahead'

1   Before you mention your ideas to anyone else ensure that you are very clear in your own mind as to why you want such a day to take place. I wanted this day to occur for two main reasons:

-   to enhance pupils' understanding of the importance of a recent historical event;
-   to develop pupils' understanding of their rights and responsibilities as citizens in a modern democracy.

2   Check with your head of department/faculty that they think it is both a good idea and practicable.

3   Discuss with other colleagues in the department/faculty and seek out their views and advice. A departmental meeting can be used to plan what needs to be done.

4   Before approaching the relevant senior manager ensure an appropriate venue is available and that your event does not clash with any other on the school calendar.

5   Once all the above has been clarified approach the appropriate senior manager/ headteacher and explain:

-   why it is such a good idea
-   why there is no practical reason why it should not take place.

6   Once you have the go ahead, advertise this day to all staff as soon as possible. They then have time to point out any potential problems and voice objections, advice and support.

Organising the day

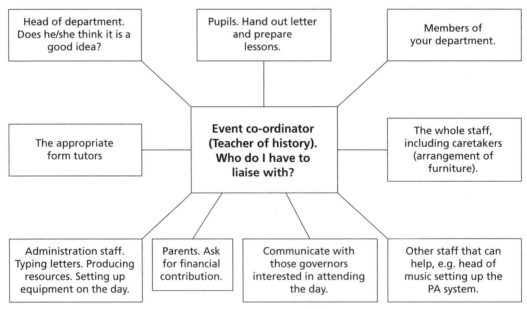

How did I publicise the event?

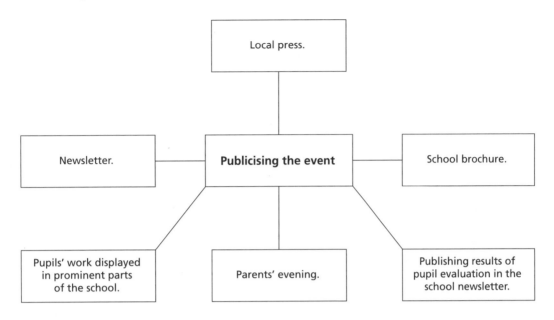

How did this day help to market citizenship?

The process of organising the day helped to raise the profile of citizenship and helped my career development. As a teacher of history, organising this day raised my profile and the status of citizenship within the department, in the faculty, and with staff in other departments, senior managers, the headteacher, governors, parents and pupils. My central role certainly helped me become the head of history within a few years. The headteacher was extremely supportive for two reasons:

- He strongly approved of the purpose of the day.
- He saw this as a good training opportunity for someone he wanted to promote to middle management. He in a sense was empowering a member of staff to organise and take decisions that would have significant implications for a whole day's learning within his school. Busher and Harris (1999: 306) refer to 'shared or devolved leadership activity where leadership activity is not chiefly the preserve of the headteacher'. This shared leadership can lead to a vibrant culture within a school where even relatively inexperienced teachers can initiate events that can enhance the curriculum.

The organisation of this day helped to develop collegiality within the department, faculty and school. Planning introductory lessons, activities during the day and follow-up lessons enabled the RE, geography and history departments to share good practice. This co-operative approach helped the Humanities Faculty to develop a greater sense of identity. Busher and Harris (1999) refer to the need for a head of department to foster collegiality by helping to shape and establish a shared vision. This collaborative approach towards planning ensured those staff involved felt empowered and valued, while the culture of shared values and sense of common direction certainly helped the Humanities Faculty to become a more coherent group that could communicate more easily and drive further initiatives. Greater sharing of pedagogy across the faculty was developed through the process of staff sitting down and planning lessons together.

This improvement in communication extended further than the Humanities Faculty. As the co-ordinator, I needed to liaise with form tutors who would be involved in supervising and chairing discussion work during the day. This helped to develop a sense of collegiality across the whole school. Busher and Harris (1999) point out that if teachers spend time together and work together, friendship groups might well develop. I would say this was the case during the process of organising and supervising this event as it enabled enthusiastic, energetic and committed teachers with a wide variety of different experiences to work together across departments towards a common goal.

Communicating to pupils what the day was about through preparatory lessons, the day itself and follow-up lessons delivered by all of the humanities departments helped them to understand that teachers could work together across departments with a shared vision. As a year group all involved in the same work at the same time, pupils talked about issues linked to the event as a year group rather than as individual classes. The pupils felt empowered as they were given the opportunity to ask questions and at the end of the process completed evaluation forms. The statistics generated by the completion of these forms were displayed within the school and published in the weekly newsletter. Pupils' work generated as a result of the day was displayed on boards in the main school reception area. Parents were sent letters before the day explaining its focus. This led to a number of them asking if they could take part during the day. At parents' evening the majority mentioned the event and were extremely positive and interested. Enthusiastic governors attended the day, taking part in discussion sessions with pupils that were held between the addresses of two guest speakers. The local press were invited to cover the event, strengthening links with the local community.

Overall, this Holocaust Memorial Day led to greater collegiality among the staff, a sense of shared purpose among an entire year group, and heightened awareness of what was going on in the school among parents, governors and the local community.

REFERENCES

Barker, B. (2005) 'Transforming Schools: Illusion or Reality?' *School Leadership and Management*, 25, 2: 99–116

Bennett, N. (1999) 'Middle Management in Secondary Schools: Introduction', *School Leadership and Management*, 19, 3: 289–92

Brundrett, M. and Terrell, I. (eds) (2004) *Learning to Lead in the Secondary School*, London: RoutledgeFalmer

Busher, H. (2005) 'Being a Middle Leader: Exploring Professional Identities', *School Leadership and Management* 25, 2: 137–53

Busher, H. and Harris, A. (1999) 'Leadership of School Subject Areas: Tensions and Dimensions of Management in the Middle', *School Leadership and Management*, 19, 3: 305–17

Davies, L., Harber, C. and Yamashita, H. (2005) *Global Citizenship Education: The Needs of Teachers and Learners*, Birmingham: Centre for International Education Research, School of Education, University of Birmingham

DfES (2004) 'The School Evaluation Tool for Citizenship Education', available at www. dfes.gov.uk/citizenship

Fleming, P. (2000) *The Art of Middle Management in Secondary Schools*, London: David Fulton

Gearon, L. (ed.) (2003) *Learning to Teach Citizenship in the Secondary School*, London: RoutledgeFalmer

Hannam, C., Smyth, P. and Stephenson, N. (1976) *The First Year of Teaching*, London: Penguin

Holden, C. (2004) '"Heaven Help the Teachers": Parents' Perspectives on the Introduction of Education for Citizenship', *Educational Review*, 56, 3: 247–58

Jackson, D. (2005)'Learning to be Teachers: Building the Confidence to Explore Global Issues', *Tidetalk*, 3: 24–5

Morrison, A. and McIntyre, D. (1969) *Teachers and Teaching*, London: Penguin

Ofsted (2002) *Inspecting Citizenship 11–16 with Guidance on Self-Evaluation*, London: 719

—— (2005) *Citizenship in Secondary Schools: Evidence from Ofsted Inspections (2003/04)* London: Ofsted

Oplatka, I., Hemsley-Brown, J. and Foskett N. (2002) 'The Voice of Teachers in Marketing Their School: Personal Perspectives in Competitive Environments', *School Leadership and Management*, 22, 2: 177–96

Potter, J. (2002) *Active Citizenship in Schools: A Good Practice Guide to Developing a Whole School Policy*, London: Kogan Page

Chapter 10 Researching citizenship

LIAM GEARON

INTRODUCTION

This chapter provides a brief outline of some recent critiques of educational research and some research contexts for citizenship education. It will not be able to focus in depth on these issues, but it will provide parameters of debate among communities of educational researchers in general and those interested in citizenship education research in particular. The questions posed, responded to and investigated by researchers in citizenship education form a small part of a wider context of educational research, and of course a relationship between citizenship and substantive disciplines which have defined its subject matter, such as the arts and humanities, economics, international relations, politics, science, etc. If debates over research priorities in citizenship education will tend naturally to vary depending upon present-day matters of import, many issues – democracy, the distribution of wealth, the environment, sustainable development, politics and governance – and educational responses to these are perennial and likely to be the focus for attention at local, national and global dimensions for the foreseeable future.

Research surveys of school curricula around the world have shown considerable international interest in citizenship education:

> During the 1990s there has been a resurgence of interest in Civic and Citizenship Education. The number of formal democracies in the world has increased from 76 (46.1%) to 117 (61.3%). This has been described as the 'third wave of democracy' related to significant world events such as the ending of apartheid in South Africa, the fall of the Berlin Wall, the democratisation of former communist states in Eastern Europe and the disintegration of the Soviet Union. Civic education programmes have become an increasingly important means for countries to educate citizens about their rights and responsibilities. Increasing pluralism within states has encouraged the development of civic education programmes that go beyond simple 'patriotic' models of citizenship requiring uncritical loyalty to the nation state. By defining 'citizenship' in terms of human rights and civic responsibilities, civic education programmes attempt to avoid concepts of 'citizenship' that define nationality in terms of ethnic, religious or cultural identity. The aspiration is that concepts of citizenship based on human rights and responsibilities may make it more difficult to mobilise political conflict around identity issues. It has therefore become the norm for modern civic education programmes to have a strong human rights values base, to make specific reference to children's rights and address issues related to diversity and the rights of minorities within society.
>
> (www.unesco.org; follow links to 'Citizenship'; accessed 17/9/05)

Teachers beginning a career in the teaching of citizenship will have come to the profession from a variety of disciplinary backgrounds. This chapter aims to consolidate previous chapters in this volume which dealt with the development of subject knowledge in citizenship and to provide a framework for the generation of new knowledge – that is, a basic outline of some research questions in citizenship – and to provide some of the parameters for this as an undertaking within educational research.

OBJECTIVES

By the end of this chapter the reader should have a grasp of:

- some basic critiques of educational research;
- some research contexts in citizenship education.

EDUCATIONAL RESEARCH

Jean-François Lyotard (1984) characterises the postmodern condition as one in which we have witnessed the end of 'grandnarratives', broad and general religious, philosophical or scientific accounts of our world. He suggests that we can no longer depend upon such grandnarratives to explain our world, in the broadest sense the human condition, and that this situation, which could be defined as a crisis of knowledge, defines the postmodern condition. In this postmodern condition, our knowledge of the world is contingent, dependent upon the particular historical and cultural contexts, and cannot be said to be universal (Popper, 1959, 1998; Sarup, 1987; Smart, 1993; Kuhn, 1996).

Of course, this is all open to challenge. In educational research, as in philosophy, the question of epistemology, of what constitutes knowledge, of how we can be sure we know what we know, remain equally critical (Berg, 2001; Cohen *et al.*, 2000; McNiff *et al.*, 2003; Robson, 2003), and equally so if we remain unclear about the ethical dimensions of that which we are investigating and the means we are using to generate new knowledge (McNamee and Bridges, 2003). Without some grasp of these underlying epistemological questions the furtherance of new knowledge can tend to be superficial, and the question of what new knowledge is in educational research is under constant scrutiny by philosophers of education (Bridges, 2003; Pring, 2004). All research therefore needs not only a grasp of some basic tools for gathering new knowledge (a method) but also a wider conceptual framework (a methodology) to place that new knowledge within a wider context of how we know what we know. In research, then, methodology is the conceptual framework wherein we seek to frame and attain knowledge of our field of research; method is the application (through practical 'tools' – interviews, surveys, philosophical reflection) whereby we seek to add to knowledge in our field of research. In research, we return constantly to the question of epistemology: what do we know and how can we be sure that we know it? Research is thus as much about presenting an understanding of the parameters in which we define such knowledge as about the knowledge we are presenting. The present-day 'crisis' in educational research is as much about a crisis in knowledge as about policy or practice.

Pring (2004) presents a succinct and authoritative eight-chapter overview of the major philosophical issues in educational research. He identifies four criticisms of educational research (see also Pring, 2000):

- Research doesn't provide governments with the information they require for decision-making on policy.
- Research doesn't help professional practice.
- Research is too often fragmented.
- Research is often tendentious or politically motivated.

The suggested solutions to this problem might be:

- Develop a cumulative body of knowledge (and especially evidence-based knowledge, including systematic research reviews).
- Develop increased involvement of professionals, like teachers, in the research process.

For the reasons outlined by Pring, under pressure from those who provide funding for research (funders want evidence that research will make a difference), current trends are towards an 'evidence-based' model in educational research. We can see this when we look at who does research, at 'communities of researchers'.

GENERIC EDUCATIONAL RESEARCH ORGANISATIONS

- British Educational Research Association (BERA). Visit www.bera.ac.uk and follow links to the downloadable reviews of research. The BERA website also shows the international dimension of research, nowhere more evident than in links to the European Education Research Association (EERA) and the American Educational Research Association (AERA).
- The Evidence for Policy and Practice Information and Co-ordinating Centre (EPPI). Visit http://eppi.ioe.ac.uk and follow links to systematic reviews.
- Philosophy of Education Society of Great Britain, www.pesgb.ac.uk. The encyclopedic references will be useful as a source of future reference, and also to demonstrate the importance of questions of philosophy and epistemology, and show that not all research has to be empirical, that without a philosophical framework, empirical research can be overly led by current-day policy concerns and may lack depth or lasting worth.

Activity 10.1

Visit one of the above-listed educational research websites. Many of the listed research communities focus on matters of importance to teachers of citizenship, such as personal and social education. BERA has an official special interest group (SIG) on social justice.

Look at the BERA website and search for the abstracts of papers presented at its annual conference (you could do the same for EERA or AERA) and download those related to research in citizenship education. One thing you might notice from such an activity is that much research of relevance to citizenship educators might not have an explicit citizenship title.

To what extent is research in citizenship education a feature of wider aspects of the work of educational researchers? Are there special issues or difficulties in researching citizenship education?

Activity 10.2

Outline a broad area of interest you might have in researching within citizenship education. If you are working in a group, share the broad areas of interest and discuss the reasons for your interest.

The critique of educational research highlighted by Pring in philosophical terms is likely to colour the educational research scene for many years to come. Ongoing discussion is found in one of the key arenas for debate, the *British Educational Research Journal*. Here, Oancea (2005) provides a detailed overview of the generic issues of policy, practice, the generation of knowledge and the general usefulness of educational research:

> The late 1990s have seen at least two discourses emerge and consolidate, one lamenting the misbehaviour of educational research from a managerial perspective (associated with a 'big science' model of knowledge production and an 'engineering' model of knowledge use), and the other attempting to defend it in the name of academic freedom and right to diversity, or to reinstate it through a humanistic model of knowledge transfer. Such allegedly antagonistic discourses about educational research are the focus of a variety of conference papers, journal editorials or book reviews . . . The role of the educational researchers is conceptualised differently, from that of a 'technician' meant to deliver answers of 'what works' to that of the 'public' or 'critical' intellectual whose accountability should be defined not in terms of immediate impact of national policies informed by research findings, but as a capacity for producing localised, transferable knowledge. Nonetheless, a worry is present that some rather anachronistic 'paradigm wars' threaten to be rekindled by pushing forward some ad hoc 'folk devils' or by 'getting the ghosts out to repeat themselves' . . . and therefore that often the deeper complexities of the matter and their philosophical underpinnings remain outside the epicentre of the debate.
>
> (Oancea, 2005: 157–8)

Oancea surveys a wealth of educational research and three key analyses of educational research: Hargreaves (1996); Tooley and Darby (1998); and Hillage *et al.* (1998). From these she presents an analysis of documents from the late twentieth century (1996–8; see also Pring, 2004) as a guide to those issues and approaches that have emerged in the twenty-first. She analyses the critiques of educational research of Hargreaves (1996), Tooley and Darby (1998) and Hillage *et al.* (1998):

- core topics/targets of criticisms;
- rhetorical devices for expressing criticism;
- philosophical themes/presuppositions

Below, by way of example, are some of the criticisms listed under 'core topics/targets of criticisms'.

SUMMARY OF CRITICISMS OF EDUCATIONAL RESEARCH FROM OANCEA'S REVIEW (2005: 166–7)

- *the commissioning of research*. The procedures for funding were criticised for being unsystematic, politically biased and based on processes, such as peer reviewing, that would exclude users' input. Also the choice of priorities was commented upon as being misdirected, uncoordinated and supply-driven;
- *the abilities, attitudes and practices of the actors involved*. The researchers were deemed guilty of insufficient training and of partisanship in the conduct and presentation of their research, in argumentation, in their choice of focus and priorities. Nonetheless, the practitioners and policy-makers, at an individual and at a collective level, were also accused of being partisan and uncoordinated, lacking interest in research, lacking ability to use research findings, and thus not offering a strong user demand for research;

- *the organisation of research* was criticised at all levels: publication – inefficient refereeing procedures, pressure to publish; networking – lack of partnership, lack of user involvement, isolation of university researchers; monitoring – incoherent, internally driven, self-validating; dissemination – linear, not targeted and inefficient, correlated with a general lack of training for using research findings and a lack of mediation; and assessment – quantitative orientation of RAE, low standards, lack of codes of good practice;
- *the methodology*. Educational research was deemed non-reliable and inconclusive. Much of this was charged to flaws of empirical research, especially qualitative – lack of triangulation, sampling bias, purposeful distortion, ideological bias, etc.; but also to flaws of non-empirical research, such as contentiousness, superficial literature review, logical incoherence, excessive reliance upon secondary sources, adulation of great thinkers;
- *the outcomes of research* were criticised in terms of presentation (omissions in reporting, imprecision, emotional language, jargon, over-theoretical language, etc.) and especially of impact of research (ineffectiveness in informing policy and practice, irrelevance for solving practical problems or for undertaken purposes, low contribution to any theoretical or methodological advancement, inaccessibility to audiences, non-cumulativity).

Oancea draws upon the notion that there is a 'new orthodoxy' in educational research:

- 'standards (model, criteria, codes) for good practice of research', 'value for money' (Tooley and Darby, 1998);
- 'body of knowledge', 'research-based profession', 'evidence-based research', 'relevance for practice', 'user involvement', 'good value for money', 'national research strategy' (Hargreaves, 1996);
- 'evidence-based policy and practice', 'strategic coherence and partnership', 'fitness for purpose', 'quality assurance', 'accessible language', 'excellence in research' (Hillage *et al.*, 1998).

One of the major drives of educational research, she concludes, then, is that educational research is increasingly driven by political necessity, and a degree of pragmatism that might *potentially* make researchers and research subject to a great extent to the behest of policy-makers, who might also fund the research. The risk is that research becomes not only lacking in independence but subject to a limited focus, because – despite the existence of research councils – only research of interest to policy-makers may receive funding.

CITIZENSHIP EDUCATION RESEARCH

Research in explicit citizenship education is as new as its post-Crick and post-National Curriculum context. What we can call implicit citizenship also has antecedents from the 1970s onwards in relatively marginal initiatives in peace education, global studies, human rights education and political education (Gearon, 2003a). With the advent of National Curriculum citizenship many of the areas previously classified under such titles shifted towards formal and explicit identification with citizenship. The most prominent review of related research at this transitional phase linked citizenship to values education and to issues around social justice in education or political education (Gearon, 2003a). The educational trend towards making citizenship *explicit* is, however, a response to dramatic changes over recent decades in the world in which we live. Increased complexity in many aspects of social and cultural, political and educational life has led to educational initiatives like citizenship. Recent international research, for example, on wider factors influencing citizenship education suggests that:

> The last two decades have witnessed a fundamental review of the concept of citizenship and what it involves in communities across the world. This review has been brought about by the impact of the rapid pace of change in modern societies in the realms of political, economic and social life and the need to respond to this impact. The pace of change is having significant influence on the nature of relationships in modern society at a number of levels, including within, between and across individuals, community groups, states, nations, regions and economic and political blocs. This period of unprecedented and seemingly relentless change has succeeded in shifting and straining the traditional, stable boundaries of citizenship in many societies. There has been particular pressure on the nature of relationships between differing groups in society as well as those between the individual and the state. The pressure has triggered a fundamental review across societies of the concepts and practices that underpin citizenship.
>
> (Kerr, 2003: 9)

A review of citizenship education across countries (Kerr, 1999a, 1999b, 2002, 2003) reveals common sets of issues and challenges that the unprecedented pace of global change was presenting to national educational systems, including:

- the rapid movement of people within and across national boundaries;
- a growing recognition of the rights of indigenous peoples and minorities;
- the collapse of existing political structures and the fledgling growth of new ones;
- the changing role and status of women in society;
- the impact of the global economy and changing patterns of work and trade on social, economic and political ties;
- the effects of the revolution in information and communications technologies;
- an increasing global population and the consequences for the environment;
- the emergence of new forms of community and protest.

(Kerr, 2003: 9)

Citizenship education, then, is an active – and at present highly transitional – response to these challenges (Gearon, 2003a, 2003c).

Activity 10.3

Given Pring's and Oancea's surveys of educational research and the problems with which it is often beset, are there issues of a similar nature for those interested in researching citizenship education? For example, does research in citizenship education risk being seen, perhaps like citizenship itself, as too closely related to government policy? Or too closely related to the problems of the day? Is this an *advantage* of research in citizenship education, in that it is perpetually relevant? Obviously this may be a very general discussion, to which you may wish to return having considered Activity 10.4.

While most research undertaken to date, with some exceptions, has been concerned with philosophical or terminological issues about the meaning and definition of citizenship in Crick and the implications of National Curriculum or syntheses of previously undertaken research (McLaughlin, 1992, 2000; Crick, 1998; QCA 1999; 2001a–g; Heater, 1999; Flew, 2000; Pearce and Hallgarten, 2000; Lawton *et al.*, 2000; Scott, 2001; Gearon, 2003a–c), increasing amounts of empirical research are available, within the UK, in Europe and globally. The role of academic researchers – who may themselves be teachers and policy-makers – is to highlight theoretical and empirical and/or evidence-based assessments of citizenship. Such research can then inform practice – in community involvement, in classrooms, in teacher training, in wider aspects of community involvement, in the light of diversity, through to policy development, and so forth (Crick, 2001; Lindsay, 2001; Jackson, 2002; Gearon, 2003a, 2003b; Maitles, 2005; Osler, 2000, 2005; Osler and Vincent, 2004; Osler and Starkey, 2006).

Crick's conceptual framework for citizenship was based upon the foundational definitions of Marshall (1950) and adapted to identify three strands in citizenship which were to prove important in its development as a National Curriculum subject: social and moral responsibility; community involvement; and political literacy. The most substantial national and international study of citizenship has been the IEA research published by NFER. This began in 1999 before citizenship was a National Curriculum subject in England. It provided an overview of approaches to citizenship education as well as a wealth of other contextual information. (Torney-Purta *et al.*, 1999; Steiner-Khamsi *et al.*, 2002). Each participating country tested and surveyed a representative national sample of fourteen-year-olds about their civic knowledge, civic concepts and attitudes, and civic engagement and participation. Kerr *et al.* (2002) include a summary of key findings:

- fourteen-year-olds in most countries, including England have an understanding of fundamental democratic values and institutions, but depth of understanding is an issue;
- there is a positive correlation between civic knowledge and participation in democratic life. Specifically, the higher students' civic knowledge, the more likely they are to participate in political and civic activities as adults;
- there is scepticism among students in England about traditional forms of political engagement, with the exception of voting. Young people are more open to other forms of involvement in civic life, such as collecting money for a social cause or participation in non-violent protests;
- schools and community organisations have untapped potential to influence the civic preparation of young people positively;
- schools that model democratic values and practices, and encourage students to discuss issues in the classroom and take an active role in the life of the school, are most effective in promoting civic knowledge and engagement. However, this approach is not the norm in many schools;
- teachers recognise the importance of citizenship education in preparing young people for citizenship;
- taken together, there is some evidence that the attitudes and beliefs of young people in the study confirm the growth of a 'new civic culture'.

In this regard citizenship education and citizenship education research are arguably unique in their subject matter, their focus often being upon the necessarily shifting context of national, regional and global political institutions and the problems which confront these. Citizenship and research into the subject provide both teacher and student with a wealth of immensely relevant and important subject matter. A timeline of the historical issues confronted and dealt with by the United Nations (how effectively is, of course, a matter of political debate) demonstrates this well: in the post-Second World War, post-Holocaust period when the United Nations was formed to counteract totalitarianism through a common model of democratic governance based on universal human rights to current-day issues of world poverty, environmental crisis and global terrorism.

ASPECTS OF CITIZENSHIP EDUCATION RESEARCH – EMERGENT CULTURAL, ECONOMIC, SOCIAL AND POLITICAL ISSUES

Visit www.un.org for a global picture of emergent cultural, economic, social and political issues among the nation states of the United Nations. A particularly useful advanced database resource for further research is the United Nations Dag Hammarskjöld Library. Again, visit www.un.org and follow links. For an authoritative independent source for international law, see the Electronic Information System for International Law (EISIL) at www.eisil.org and follow links.

Activity 10.4

- Visit the UN website. What are main areas of concern for the UN? Are there any areas of particular relevance to education? Or to citizenship education in particular?
- Visit the UNESCO website to see how the political concerns of the UN are translated into educational programmes for curriculum development and research.
- Devise a research task for pupils to investigate an aspect of global importance in the UN system, and with relevance to the local school community.

Activity 10.5

Refer to Activity 10.2, above. Try to refine your broad area of interest into a specific research *question*. For example, 'What is the extent of pupils' knowledge and understanding of the United Nations [or UNESCO, or the Commonwealth, or the European Union, or the Council of Europe, etc.]?'

Educational research is a technical and complex process, integrally connected to the pursuit of new knowledge and thus to epistemological questions about what constitutes new (or any) knowledge. Educational research is closely related to the social sciences but not all educational research is empirical; some will be philosophical.

Use one of the standard textbooks on educational research (for instance, Robson, 2003; Cohen *et al.*, 2000), and consider what method (questionnaire, survey, interview, etc.) you might use in order to investigate your research question. Use Ian Davies's guide 'Research' in the Citized induction pack (see box below) to see whether there is any possibility of developing the idea further.

There is an increasing amount of research being undertaken today on issues of critical significance and importance to both national and international communities as well as citizenship education, including, for instance, a major study at the National Foundation for Educational Research (NFER) 'Citizenship Education: Longitudinal Study in England' (from 2001 to 2009, with the first report published in 2002, and the 2005 report surveying a pupil cohort of 6,400; see www.nfer.ac.uk and follow links). The political problems of history as well as those of the present day are potential subjects for citizenship education research. The box below provides a selective list of some key hubs of information, from lists of academic resources for undertaking research and organisations that use research in citizenship to organisations that undertake citizenship education research.

CITIZENSHIP EDUCATION AND CITIZENSHIP EDUCATION RESEARCH

UK-based

BeCaL

The BeCaL Bibliography is a collection of academic sources (paper, abstracts, related references) in values education, including citizenship education. The BeCaL Database is part of the Values, Education and Learning Gateway; visit www.becal.org.uk.

Citized

The website www.citized.info (follow links) provides a major source of current information on citizenship in initial teacher training. The induction pack provides a systematic range of resources for all aspects of citizenship teaching and training:

TEACHING UNITS

Citizenship Education for Sustainable Development in Initial Teacher Training
Community & Diverse Communities – Andrew Peterson
Community Action for Sustainable Development – John Huckle
Ethics and Tolerance – Robert Bowie
Global Conflict – Ian Davies
Justice and the Law – Andrew Peterson
Schools Councils – Ian Davies

ITT PROGRAMMES

Citizenship – Subject Knowledge – Peter Brett
Effective Transition KS2–KS3 – Hilary Claire and Cathie Holden
Making Citizenship Teacher Education Courses Become More Active and Participative – Janet Palmer
Post 14 Citizenship Examinations – Ralph Leighton
Standards Relevant to the Achievement of Qualified Teacher Status in Citizenship – Ian Davies
Subject Co-ordination for Citizenship Education – Lynn Revell

THEME: RESEARCH

Applying for External Funding – Ian Davies
Higher Degrees – Ian Davies

THEME: RESOURCES

Citizenship Organisations and Resources – Roma Woodhead
Resources for Teaching Citizenship: A Guide for Beginning Teachers of Citizenship – Peter Brett
The theme of 'Research' is obviously most relevant to this chapter but research requires an integrated approach to the development of knowledge, such as is possible.

British Educational Research Association

Visit the BERA website, www.bera.ac.uk, and look for systematic reviews relevant to citizenship, including Gearon (2003a).

Economic and Social Research Council

The ESRC, www.esrc.ac.uk, is the major funding council for economic and social research in the UK, and has citizenship as a significant strand in its funding priorities.

Evidence for Policy and Practice Co-ordinating Centre

EPPI is based at the Institute of Education. It has undertaken systematic reviews of empirical research in citizenship education and is a most useful hub for research; visit http://eppi.ioe.ac.uk

National Foundation for Educational Research (NFER)

Visit www.nfer.ac.uk and follow links. NFER is a major funding organisation and undertaker of educational research.

Qualifications and Curriculum Authority (QCA, UK)

The website, www.qca.org.uk, contains links to curriculum material, including National Curriculum citizenship.

Teachernet

The website, www.teachernet.org.uk, has extensive reference points for curriculum development rather than research but it is still useful.

Journals

Generic journals of educational research are too numerous to list but those associated with professional educational research are important. Specific to citizenship education research: *Education, Citizenship and Social Justice* (see www.sagepublications.com and follow links); *International Journal of Citizenship and Teacher Education* (see www.citized.info and follow links); *Reflecting Education* (see www.reflectingeducation.net and follow links; volume 1, number 3 is dedicated to citizenship).

Europe-wide

Council of Europe

This body declared 2005 the European Year of Citizenship through Education, and its website provides a Europe-wide resource of recent research in citizenship and education for democratic citizenship (EDC); visit www.coe.int/edc and follow links.

European Union

The newly expanded European Union has, like the Council of Europe, a considerable interest in harmonising notions of European identity, and thus prioritising notions of citizenship across its member states; visit http://europa.eu.int/and follow links.

EURYDICE

The website www.eurydice.org provides an excellent resource for empirical research across Europe.

US-based and worldwide

INTERNATIONAL ASSOCIATION FOR THE EVALUATION OF EDUCATIONAL ACHIEVEMENT (IEA)

IEA (2004) *Civic Knowledge and Engagement at Age 14 in 28 Countries: Results from the IEA Civic Education Study* by Judith Torney-Purta, Jo-Ann Amadeo and Rainer Lehmann; the most important worldwide source for citizenship or civics education research, with links at www.indiana.edu and www.iea.nl.

UNITED NATIONS

The website www.un.org is one of the most underused resources in global education, superb for all issues in citizenship, including economics, environment and global terrorism, and outstanding as a resource on human rights. Responses by nation states to the UN's International Decade for Human Rights Education, including curricula incorporating citizenship and human rights, can be found at http://ap.ohchr.org/documents.

UNESCO

The website www.unesco.org, another highly usable resource, has much specific work on citizenship education research.

USERS OF RESEARCH: PROFESSIONAL ORGANISATIONS)

- Citized (www.citized.info)
- Citizenship Foundation (www.citizenshipfoundation.org.uk)
- Institute for Citizenship (www.ifc.org.uk)

Activity 10.6

Discussion: In the light of Activities 10.1–5, discuss how research might be used in developing the quality of classroom teaching in citizenship education.

SUMMARY

Citizenship education research globally is at an important stage in its development. Research in citizenship education will need to address many of the challenges posed within and raised by educational research; the wider political significance of research in citizenship might yet make a contribution to more general debates on the usefulness of education research.

REFERENCES

Arthur, J., Davison, J. and Stow, W. (2000) *Social Literacy, Citizenship Education and the National Curriculum*, Canterbury: Canterbury Christ Church University.

Berg, B.L. (2001) *Qualitative Research Methods for the Social Sciences*, 4th edn, Boston: Allyn and Bacon.

Bridges, D. (2003) *Fiction Written under Oath? Essays in Philosophy and Educational Research*, London: Kluwer Academic.

Clark, C. (2005) 'The structure of educational research', *British Educational Research Journal* 31, 3: 289–309.

Cohen, L., Manion, L. and Morrison, K. (2000) *Research Methods in Education*, 5th edn, London: RoutledgeFalmer.

Cogan, J. and Derricott, R. (1998) *Citizenship for the 21st Century*, London: Kogan Page.

Crick, B. (1998) *Education for Citizenship and the Teaching of Democracy in Schools: Final Report of the Advisory Group on Citizenship*, London: QCA.

—— (ed.) (2001) *Citizens: Towards a Citizenship Culture*, Oxford: Blackwell.

Flew, A. (2000) *Education for Citizenship*, London: IEA Studies in Education.

Gearon, L. (2003a) *How Do We Learn to Become Good Citizens?: A Professional User Review of UK Research*, London: British Educational Research Association.

—— (2003b) *The Human Rights Handbook: A Global Perspective for Education*, Stoke-on-Trent and Sterling, VA: Trentham.

—— (ed.) (2003c) *Learning to Teach Citizenship in the Secondary School*, London: Routledge.

Hammersley, M. (2002) *Educational Research, Policymaking and Practice*, London: Paul Chapman.

—— (2005) 'Countering the "new orthodoxy" in educational research: a response to Phil Hodkinson', *British Educational Research Journal* 31, 2: 139–55.

Hargreaves, D.H. (1996) 'Teaching as a Research Based Profession: Possibilities and Prospects', Teacher Training Agency Annual Lecture, London.

Heater, D. (1999) *What is Citizenship?* Cambridge: Polity Press.

Hillage, J., Pearson, R., Anderson, A. and Tamkin, P. (1998) *Excellence in Research on Schools*, report for the Department for Education and Employment, London: DfEE.

Jackson, R. (2002) *International Perspectives on Citizenship, Education and Religious Diversity*, London: Routledge.

Kerr, D. (1999a) *Re-examining Citizenship Education: The Case of England*, Slough: NFER.

—— (1999b) *Citizenship Education: An International Comparison*, London: QCA/NFER.

—— (2000) 'The Making of Citizenship in the National Curriculum (England): Issues and Challenges', paper presented at European Conference on Educational Research (ECER), University of Edinburgh, 22 September.

—— (2002). 'An international review of citizenship in the curriculum: the IEA national case studies and the INCA archive', in G. Steiner-Khamsi, J. Torney-Purta and J. Schwille (eds), *New Paradigms and Recurring Paradoxes in Education for Citizenship*, Amsterdam: Elsevier Press.

—— (2003) 'Citizenship education in international perspective', in L. Gearon (ed.), *Learning to Teach Citizenship in the Secondary School*, London: Routledge.

Kerr, D., Lines, A., Blenkinsop, S. and Schagen, I. (2001) *Citizenship and Education at Age 14: A Summary of the International Findings and Preliminary Results for England*, Slough: NFER.

Kerr, D., Lines, A., Blenkinsop, S. and Schagen, I. (2002) *What Citizenship and Education Mean to 14-Year-Olds: England's Results from the IEA Citizenship Education Study*, London: DfES/NFER.

Kuhn, T. (1996) *The Structure of Scientific Revolutions*, 3rd edn, Chicago: Chicago University Press.

Lawton, D., Cairns, J. and Gardner, R. (2000) *Education for Citizenship*, London: Continuum.

Lindsay, I. (2001) 'The voluntary sector', in B. Crick (ed.), *Citizens: Towards a Citizenship Culture*, Oxford: Blackwell.

Lyotard, J.-F. (1984) *The Postmodern Condition: An Enquiry into Knowledge*, Manchester: Manchester University Press.

McLaughlin, T.H. (1992) 'Citizenship, diversity and education: a philosophical perspective', *Journal of Moral Education* 21, 3: 235–50.

—— (2000) 'Citizenship education in England: the Crick Report and beyond', *Journal of Philosophy of Education* 34, 4: 541–70.

McNamee, M. and Bridges, D. (eds) (2003) *Ethics and Educational Research*, Oxford: Blackwell.

McNiff, J. Lomax, P. and White, J. (2003) *You and Your Action Research Project*, 2nd edn, London: RoutledgeFalmer.

Maitles, H. (2005) *Values in Education – We're all Citizens Now*, Edinburgh: Dunedin Academic Press.

Marshall, T.H. (1950) *Social Class and Citizenship*, Cambridge: Cambridge University Press.

Nash, N. (2005) 'Explanation and quantification in educational research: the arguments of critical and scientific realism', *British Educational Research Journal* 31, 2: 185–204.

NFER (2005) 'Citizenship Education: Longitudinal Study in England', available at: www.nfer.ac.uk.

NFER/DfEE (2002) *Citizenship Education: Longitudinal Study, 2002–2009*, Slough: NFER.

Oancea, A. (2005) 'Criticisms of educational research: key topics and levels of analysis', *British Educational Research Journal* 31, 2: 157–84.

Osler, A. (2005) *Teachers, Human Rights and Diversity*, Stoke-on-Trent: Trentham Books.

—— (ed.)) (2000) *Citizenship and Democracy in Schools: Diversity, Identity, Equality*, Stoke-on-Trent: Trentham Books.

Osler, A. and Starkey, H. (2006) *Education For Democratic Citizenship: A Review of Research, Policy and Practice 1995–2005*, London: British Educational Research Association.

Osler, A. and Vincent, K. (2004) *Citizenship and the Challenge of Global Education*, Stoke-on-Trent: Trentham.

Pearce, N. and Hallgarten, P. (2000) *Tomorrow's Citizens*, London: IPPR.

Popper, K. (1959) *The Logic of Scientific Discovery*, Oxford: Oxford University Press.

—— (1998) *Unended Quest*, London: Routledge.

Pring, R. (2000) 'The 'false dualism' of educational research', *Journal of Philosophy of Education* 34, 2: 247–60.

—— (2004) *Philosophy of Education Research*, 2nd edn, London and New York: Continuum.

QCA (1999) *National Curriculum Handbooks for Primary and Secondary Teachers*, London: Qualifications and Curriculum Authority.

—— (2001a) *Citizenship: A Scheme of Work for Key Stage 3*, London: Qualifications and Curriculum Authority.

—— (2001b) *Citizenship: A Scheme of Work for Key Stage 4*, London: Qualifications and Curriculum Authority.

—— (2001c) *Citizenship: A Scheme of Work for Key Stage 3: Teacher's Guide*, London: Qualifications and Curriculum Authority.

—— (2001d) *Citizenship: A Scheme of Work for Key Stage 4: Teacher's Guide*, London: Qualifications and Curriculum Authority.

—— (2001e) *Citizenship: Key Stages 3–4*, London: Qualifications and Curriculum Authority).

—— (2001f) *Getting Involved: Extending Opportunities for Pupil Participation (KS3)*, London: Qualifications and Curriculum Authority.

—— (2001g) *Staying Involved: Extending Opportunities for Pupil Participation (KS4)*, London: Qualifications and Curriculum Authority.

Robson, C. (2003) *Real World Research: A Resource for Social Scientists and Practitioner-Researchers*, 2nd edn, Oxford: Blackwell.

Sarup, M. (1987) *An Introductory Guide to Post-Structuralism and Postmodernism*, 2nd edn, Athens, GA: University of Georgia Press.

Scott, D. (ed.) (2001) *Curriculum Journal*, 11, special issue: 'Responses to Crick'.

Smart, B. (1993) *Postmodernity*, London: Routledge.

Steiner-Khamsi, G., Torney-Purta, J. and Schwille, J. (eds) (2002) *New Paradigms and Recurring Paradoxes in Education for Citizenship*, Amsterdam: Elsevier Press.

Tooley, J. and Darby, D. (1998) *Educational Research: A Critique of Published Educational Research*, report for the Office for Standards in Education, London: Ofsted.

Torney-Purta, J., Schwille, J. and Amadeo, J.-A. (eds) (1999) *Civic Education across Countries: 24 Case Studies from the IEA Civic Education Project*, Amsterdam: International Association for the Evaluation of Educational Achievement (IEA).

Torney-Purta, J., Lehmann, R., Oswald, H. and Schulz, W. (2001) *Citizenship and Education in Twenty-eight Countries: Civic Knowledge and Participation at Age Fourteen*, Amsterdam: International Association for the Evaluation of Educational Achievement (IEA).

Appendix to Chapter 3

CITIZENSHIP AT GCSE AND A LEVEL – AQA AND OCR SUBJECT CONTENT

	AQA Short GCSE course in Citizenship Studies (2006–7)	OCR Short GCSE course in Citizenship Studies	AQA Advanced subsidiary GCE in Social Science: Citizenship
	www.aqa.org.uk	www.ocr.org.uk	www.aqa.org.uk
The Nature of Citizenship			Definitions of citizenship, and contemporary debates about the citizen in the modern state. Individualist and communitarian views of citizenship. The changing nature of ideologies of conservatism, liberalism and socialism, including the concept of post-ideological politics. The extent to which such ideas are used to frame contemporary debates about citizenship.
Conflict Resolution	Issues relating to one current area of international conflict or co-operation.	Dealing with conflict through responsible voluntary action, and other processes of bringing about social change. Key points of one topical international conflict.	Sources of power and authority in groups; decision-making; strategies for resolving conflict and achieving collaboration, both formal (e.g., voting), and informal (e.g., persuasion and negotiation).
Community	How power and authority are exercised within school.	Interdependence and mutual respect between individuals and	Community and individual responsibility. Influence of socialisation

	How schools can promote equal opportunities and reflect the diverse multicultural nature of society.	communities. Processes of change within communities, and the role of individuals and groups in bringing about social change. Formal and informal processes of meeting local needs. Discrimination and its social and legal implications.	in creating differently empowered citizens. Differences in life-chances in relation to health, education and employment. Anti-discrimination policies and equal opportunities. Individual, structural and cultural explanations of poverty and inequality; consequences for citizens, families and society.
Culture and Race	How ethnic identity, culture and religion can affect community life.	How rights and responsibilities are viewed within different cultures. The nature of ethnic, religious, national and regional identities.	Influences on voting behaviour such as class, age, ethnicity, gender, religion and region. The influence of class, gender, sexuality, ethnicity, age and nationality on both participation in society and the construction of a citizen's identity.
Business and Economics	Legal and moral rights and responsibilities of employers and employees. How a case study or work experience company relates to other businesses and contributes to the local and national economy. How individuals and businesses use financial services.	Consumer rights and responsibilities. Employer and employee rights and responsibilities. Employer and employee organisations. Fair and unfair trade.	
Human Rights	Moral and legal rights and responsibilities of parents, teachers and students. Issues of disputed human rights	Rights and responsibilities in school/college. International human rights.	The citizen's legal, political and social rights. Universal rights and duties. Civil liberties in Britain, Europe and globally. Human Rights Act. Freedom of information.
Crime, Justice and the Law	Young people and the law, including consumer, race relations, human rights and age-related legislation. How laws are made and how courts use the law. Criminal and civil law. The role of police, magistrates, solicitors, barristers, judges and juries.	Criminal and civil law. Criminal and civil courts. How courts interpret the law.	The courts and alternatives such as ADR, tribunals, ombudsmen. The legal profession, advice and representation. The citizen's voice in legal process. The rights of the police and the accused. The prosecution process. Law enforcement – uses and dangers.
The Voluntary Sector	How individuals can bring about change	The role of self-help groups, special interest	The private and voluntary sectors.

	through voluntary organisations.	groups, charities and community groups. Arguments for and against aid from richer to poorer countries.	Examples of local action (such as self-help) which may enhance social inclusion, or local pressure groups which may support local community interests – e.g., the local environment.
Parliament and Democracy	Power and authority at local, national and devolved governmental levels. Referendums, elections and participation in political parties.	The relationship between government and Parliament. How bills become law. Universal suffrage, rights and responsibilities to take part in elections. Regional parliaments and assemblies in the UK.	Theories and forms of representation: elections, manifestos and the mandate. Powers and main responsibilities of elected representatives, from parish, district and county councillors to MPs and MEPs.
Media in Society	The importance of a free press. The responsibilities of the media. Media and formation of public opinion.	Culture and the media. Law and the media. Politics and the media. Government and the media. Global issues and the media. The role of the media and the internet in international affairs.	Elected representatives' interaction with the media. Use of the media and the internet to influence voting behaviour. The use of the media in campaigning on local, national or global issues. Local, national and global influences of the media: competing debates and models such as consensus and pluralist. Agenda setting and the issue of bias. The processes of labelling and stereotyping in the media.
Government and Public Services	How government exercises power, authority and responsibility in managing the economy, raising taxes and funding public services.	Government responsibilities for the economy and public services. Local and national taxes. The public and the private sectors.	Debates about welfare and the state. Housing, health care, provision for the old. The Citizen's Charter; aims and effectiveness. Citizens as public service consumers. The main functions and levels of government, local to European.
The UN and Commonwealth	Relationships between the UK, the UN and the Commonwealth, and associated rights and responsibilities.	The nature of the Commonwealth. The nature of the UN, and the UK's role within it.	
The Global Community	Global inequality, trading practices, multinational companies and aid. Global interdependence.	The nature of global dependence and interdependence. Responsibilities of citizens	

	How consumers, the media, pressure groups and governments can influence international issues.	towards global issues. Thinking globally, acting locally to bring about change. Key points of one topical international issue.	
Europe	Power and authority at European governmental level. Relationships between the UK and the EU and associated rights and responsibilities.	The EU and its relationship with the UK.	
ESD (Education for sustainable development)	The nature of sustainable development. Local Agenda 21.	The nature of sustainable development. Local Agenda 21.	
Active Citizenship	Ways in which schools can provide opportunities for student participation and community involvement. How individuals can bring about change through democratic processes, pressure groups or voluntary organisations.	How individuals can take part in democratic processes – e.g., school councils, pressure groups, political parties. Processes of responsible voluntary action, including planning, communication, negotiation, participation and evaluation.	Membership of political parties and pressure groups. Attending meetings, voting, campaigning, fundraising. Parliamentary action (writing to MPs, lobbying) and extra-parliamentary action (using the media, campaigning, demonstrating). Knowledge of the aims, methods and effectiveness of a local, national, European or worldwide campaign which has sought to promote a particular policy and/or influence a political decision (e.g.,road building, GM crops, global warming).

Index